INSTRUCTOR'S MANUAL

GLOBAL MANAGEMENT

Mark Mendenhall
University of Tennessee, Chattanooga

Betty Jane Punnett
University of Windsor

David Ricks
American Graduate School of
International Management, Thunderbird

Prepared by Carolan McLarney and Edward Chung

ISBN 1-55786-677-5

BLACKWELL
Cambridge MA & Oxford UK

Printed in the United States of America.

ISBN: 1-55786-677-5

<u>**CONTENTS**</u>

Carolan McLarney would like to thank her parents and brother for their faith and support.

Ed Chung thanks Jan for each of the last 22 years, and for Chester and Norman.

Part I: Introduction

This Instructor's Manual has been designed to present you with a complete teaching package. We have included a sample course outline, comprehensive lecture outlines to be used with each chapter in the textbook, and a test bank of questions for each chapter. Each of the chapters of the book builds upon the previous to form an integrated approach to global management. In order for the student to gain a full understanding of global management, they must have a thorough knowledge of the previous chapters. We have found that most of our students like this integrated approach of the text material and course concepts; the quality of class discussions on the conceptual frameworks is much improved and we believe that this is due in part to the experiential exercise and case discussions.

This text is primarily intended for use in an introductory International Management course, usually taught at the second or third year level in an undergraduate program. We believe that the style and material is appropriate for this level because we have tried to ensure that the material covered is readable and easy to understand, and yet it covers the topics in some depth. Many professors will find the text appropriate for a more advanced, or graduate, course as well. Professors who use the text at this level can supplement it with additional readings. The level at which the text is used will determine, to a large extent, the way in which it will be used. For example:

(a) If it is used at an **introductory** level (i.e. community college or first year university), then the instructor will likely spend much of the term covering the material in the chapters in a lecture format. The discussion of questions, case analysis, outside readings, etc. will make up a relatively minor aspect of the course.

(b) If it is used at an **intermediate** level (i.e. second or third year university), then the instructor will likely divide the time relatively evenly between going over the material in the chapters and discussion questions and so on.

(c) If it is used at an **advanced** level (i.e. fourth year university or graduate level), then the text material can provide the basis for discussion and more advanced readings. In this case, the instructor will likely not go over the material in the chapters, except where it is felt to be particularly unfamiliar to students, and will devote most time to discussion questions and so on.

Each professor, of course, has a unique style and these general comments will be adapted to each particular style. This is equally true of the discussion that makes up the balance of this instructor's manual. Our aim in preparing this manual was to make the use of the text as rewarding an experience as possible. We do not attempt to provide a model for teaching your course, but instead, provide suggestions from which you can select those which best serve your needs. There are many different factors which may have an impact on the format of a particular course, including: class size and level, room layout, term length, regulations governing testing and marking, and the professor's and students' preferences. Our suggestions are, therefore, often general in nature and you will want to adapt them for your particular course.

The test bank provides a variety of types of questions. Answers to the multiple choice and true or false questions are indicated in **bold** with the question. The page number indicating where the material on which the question is based follows each answer. Page numbers for materials related to the short essay questions are indicated with the question. The choice of question type, as well as the specific questions used, will depend on the course being offered. We have tried to provide complete coverage of topics and a wide variety of questions so that professors can select from these.

In preparing this manual, we started with the question: *"What do we want in the manual?"* We reviewed other instructors manuals and noted those aspects which we found particularly helpful. The material in this manual reflects our answer to the question. We have provided you with a sample course outline, comments on teaching approaches, suggestions for additional materials, and specific comments on each chapter of the text. The chapter comments do not revisit the material found in the chapter, but rather they provide a chapter summary, suggested class agenda, and answers to the discussion questions.

Part II: Sample Course Outline

There are many factors that affect the specific design of a course. We have decided to provide you with a typical course outline used by one of the authors, rather than provide a variety of outlines to fit many different needs. This outline serves to identify the components of the course and approximate time allocated to each chapter. This can be used as the basis for designing an outline to fit your specific needs and time constraints

---

Course #

Introduction to International Management
Fall 199X

Monday and Wednesday 8:30 to 11:20 am

Instructor:

Office: Office #
Business Building
Faculty of Business Adminstration

Telephone: (xxx) XXX-XXXX

Office Hours: Monday and Wednesday 1:0-2:30 pm

If you are unable to meet me during normal office hours please feel free to make an appointment to see me at another time.

Course Overview:

The focus of this course is on the management of international businesses or multinational companies (MNCs). The fact that international businesses operate in different nations means that they must operate within the context of varied national requirements and cultural expectations. The aim of this course is to investigate how these differences affect the management of enterprises that are international.

The course is essentially a survey course, therefore, it considers many aspects of management internationally. A broad range of topics are covered but there is no time to address them all in depth. The purpose here is to expose you to a variety of topics so that you may pursue those of particular interest in greater depth at a later date.

This course consists of four major components:

1.   The Global Picture: Understanding the International Management Environment.

2.   The Firm Picture: Understanding Strategic Management and Operations.

3.   The People Picture: Executing International Decisions through Staffing and Directing

4.   Application of Concepts, Models and Theories - Using Assignments, Cases, Exercises, and so on.

Textbooks:

The following textbooks have been ordered by the campus bookstore:

Mendenhall, M., Punnett, B.J. & D. Ricks,   Global Management, Cambridge: Blackwell, 1994.
   (This text will be identified in the Class Schedule as **GM**)

Punnett, B.J.,   Experiencing International Business and Management, Wadsworth Publishing, 1994.
   (This text will be identified in the Class Schedule as **EIM**)

Ricks, D.,   Blunders in International Business, Cambridge, Mass: Blackwell Publishers, 1993.

The following textbooks have been placed on reserve in the Business Library:

Copeland, L. & L. Griggs,   Going International, New York: New American Library, 1985.

Porter, M.,   The Competitive Advantage of Nations, New York: The Free Press, 1990.

Class Schedule:

If changes are required to this schedule, they will be identified and the schedule amended by the end of the second week of the semester.

Week	Topics	Assignments
Week 1: Mnth/Day	Introduction & Overview History	<u>Text</u>: Chapter 1 **(GM)** <u>Assignment</u>: Identify and discuss a current issue of importance to Global Management (hand in 1 page analysis)
Week 2: Month/Day	The Political Environment	<u>Text</u>: Chapter 2 **(GM)** <u>Exercise</u>: Integrative Case
Week 3: Month/Day	The Cultural Environment (Guest Lecturer on Monday)	<u>Text</u>: Chapter 3 **(GM)** <u>Movie</u>: "Kacho" <u>Exercise</u>: #7 **(EIM)**
Week 4: Month/Day	The Labour Environment The Ethical Environment	<u>Text</u>: Chapters 4, 5 **(GM)**
Week 5: Month/Day	International Strategy Overview	<u>Text</u>: Chapter 6 **(GM)** <u>Movie</u>: "Going International"
Week 6: Month/Day	The Foreign Entry Decision	<u>Text</u>: Chapter 7 **(GM)** ***TEST ON WEDNESDAY*** (Chapters 1 to 7)
Week 7: Month/Day	Implementing Foreign Entry Decisions Adapting Management Practices	<u>Text</u>: Chapter 8 **(GM)** Chapter 9 **(GM)**

Week	Topics	Assignments
Week 8: Month/Day	Operations Management in International Organizations	<u>Text:</u> Chapter 10 (**GM**) <u>Movie:</u> "McDonald's in Moscow" <u>Presentations:</u> Group #1 (Mon) Group #2 (Wed)
Week 9: Month/Day	Organizing and Control in International Organizations	<u>Text:</u> Chapter 11 (**GM**) <u>Exercise:</u> Integrative Case <u>Presentations:</u> Group #3 (Mon) Group #4 (Wed)
Week 10: Month/Day	Personnel Selection for International Assignments Training for International Assignments	<u>Text:</u> Chapters 12, 13 (**GM**) <u>Exercise:</u> #4 (**EIM**) <u>Presentations:</u> Group #5 (Mon) Group #6 (Wed)
Week 11: Month/Day	Managing the Expatriate Manager	<u>Text:</u> Chapter 14 (**GM**) <u>Presentations:</u> Group #7 (Mon) Group #8 (Wed)
Week 12: Month/Day	Special Issues: Women & Dual-Career Couples *TEST*	<u>Text:</u> Chapter 15 (**GM**) *TEST ON MONDAY !* (Chapters 8 to 17) <u>Presentations:</u> Group #9 (Wed)
Week 13: Month/Day	Communication and Negotiation Leadership and Motivation Poster Session	<u>Text:</u> Chapters 16, 17 (**GM**) <u>Presentations:</u> Group #10 (Mon) <u>Poster Session:</u> Wednesday

Grades:

Tests	30%
Assignments	20%
Country Poster	5%
Group Assignment	15%
Final Examination	30%

<u>Tests:</u>   Tests will be multiple choice and short essay format. They will be based on the assigned readings and class discussions.

<u>Assignments:</u> The assignments are as follows -
(1 X 2%)   1. One page analysis of current issues.
(3 X 2%)   2. Discussion/analysis of three discussion
                              questions (**) (** the discussion questions are found at
                         the end of each chapter. Each student is required to submit
                         answers to three discussion questions of their choice over the
                         course of the semester)
(1 X 12%)   3. Two integrative cases will be discussed in the semester, each
                         student will select one of these cases and prepare an analysis.

<u>Country Poster:</u> Each student will select a country and prepare a poster with business-related information. These posters will be presented to other students during a poster session.

<u>Group Assignment:</u> Groups of approximately four people will be formed to work on a project together. These projects are intended to simulate real decisions that you might be asked to make in an international company. You will research your chosen topic and present your findings to the class. Your presentation will last about thirty minutes. A written paper will be handed in which will summarize your presentation and include background materials not included in the oral presentation. Grades will be based on the content of the presentation as well as the clarity and interest of the presentation. Class members will be asked to rate each presentation and these peer evaluations will be taken into account in grading presentations. Suggested group presentation topics are listed below, if you have a different topic which you would like to address we can consider it. Please form a group, select a topic and choose a presentation date as soon as possible. The earlier that you make your choice, the more likely it is that you will get your first choice. Students who are not a part of a group by the end of the third week will be assigned a group.

Potential Topics for the Group Assignment:

Part One - The Global Picture

Political Analysis of a Country
Political Risk Analysis: a Particular Company's Perspective
Cultural Analysis of a Country
Comparison of Two Countries in Terms of Politics or Culture
Comparisons of Labor Relations in Two Contrasting Countries
Discuss Recent Ethical Dilemmas Faced by Global Companies

Part Two - The Firm Picture

Select a Firm, Assess its Global Competitive Advantages
Discuss Exporting a Product to a Foreign Location
Discuss Investing in a Specific Foreign Location
Examine Changes in Management Relative to a Cultural Model
Identify Exports and Imports of Goods and Services from a Strategic Operations Perspective
Identify and Discuss Global Organizational Structure for a Specific Firm

Part Three - The People Picture

Develop a Selection and Training Program for Employees for a Specific Foreign Country
Develop a Negotiation Plan for a Foreign Country
Discuss Issues Faced by a Woman Manager in a Muslim Country
Develop a Plan for Male Spouses on a Foreign Assignment
Contrast Leadership Styles in Two Countries
Select a High Context Country and a Low Context Country and Compare Communication Styles

Other

Consideration of the effect of the N.A.F.T.A. on a particular company or industry
Examination of opportunities arising from recent events in
    Eastern Europe
    the European Community
    South Africa

<u>Final Examination:</u> The final examination will be held during the scheduled examination slot. A case will be distributed in advance for your analysis, and the examination will consist of a series of questions relating to the case. It will be an open book examination and its intent is to have you apply concepts from the class to a real situation. Grades will be based upon your apparent understanding of the concepts and your ability to apply them logically and realistically.

Part III: Additional Materials

1. Experiential Materials:

These provide simulations of real-life experiences. Currently only a limited amount of complementary material is available. These are some of which we are aware:

Experiencing International Management by B.J. Punnett, Wadsworth, 1993.

This text contains a series of exercises and projects which simulate real international situations. Students can complete some in class, others require outside preparation. The topic covered correspond, to a large degree, with those covered in the text.

Bafa Bafa from Simile III, 218-12th Street, DalMar, California, U.S.A. 92014. Tele: (629) 755-0272.

This excellent simulation of two contrasting cultures enables students to experience culture shock and explore issues of ethnocentrism.

Country Profiles

These can be used to create a variety of experiential situations. Profiles are available from the State Department as well as from a variety of Banks for selected countries. Country profiles are included in **Experiencing International Management**, and these can be used to familiarize students with a variety of countries. Students can be asked to update the information on these profiles - this provides good experience in finding and synthesizing information from a variety of sources, as well as illustrating the changes which occur over time (Yugoslavia is a particularly startling example).

2. Films (Movies and Videos):

These provide a visual supplement to other course materials. There are three films we have used regularly and believe that they would be appropriate in most courses. They are:

    (a) **Going International** (Parts I-IV)
    (b) **KACHO** (Japan)
    (c) **McDonald's in Moscow**

Most professors will want to identify films of particular relevance to their specific class, therefore, we offer the following suggestions for identifying available films. Your College or University likely has films and videos available through the Media Centre or Library. It is always a good idea to begin by considering these. Those used in other business courses are sometimes helpful, and in many cases, films or videos used by other areas may be of interest in an International Management Course. We have found films used in Anthropology, Communications Studies, Economics, Political Science, Sociology, and Religious Studies to be useful. In addition, films used in various Area Studies Programs (i.e. Asian Studies, Canada-U.S. Studies, European Studies, Japan Studies, Latin American Studies, etc...) have provided valuable information.

The following organizations may be contacted to see what they may have available through their offices. These films are often available free of charge or for a minimal cost.

    (a) Trade and Industry Associations
    (b) Federal and State or Provincial Departments of Commerce, Industry and Trade
    (c) Trade Representatives of Foreign Governments
    (d) Public Television Stations

Commercial distributors of films can also be contacted. They should be easy to identify through the Yellow Pages. These films may be expensive, but in many cases their purchase is warranted if they will be used for several years. These distributors can usually provide an extensive catalogue, and the films are available for preview. If cost is a concern, consider other areas of the college and university, such as those mentioned as sources of films, that might also use a particular film and see if the cost can be shared.

3. Additional Readings:

There are many International Business textbooks available and some International/Global Management texts. It is a good idea to ensure that a variety of these are available to students, usually by placing them on reserve in the library. Because each textbook presents material in its own unique manner, and because different texts include material not included in others, it is often helpful for students to refer to other texts. There are other books available which you want to consider; particularly those with a particular regional focus (i.e. doing business in China) or a specific aim (i.e. advice for expatriates). There are other books as well which are of interest to students. These books present material in a format which students find interesting and easy to read. They provide a good counterpoint to the more traditional textbook used in most courses. Two books which we have found most useful are:

Copeland, L. & L. Griggs. **Going International**, New York: New American Library, 1985.

> This book provides a practical perspective on doing business internationally. It is relatively short and includes material which students find interesting and informative.

Axtell, R.E., **Do's and Taboos of Hosting International Visitors**, New York: John Wiley & Sons, 1990.

> This book provides a practical and informative guide for Americans hosting foreign business colleagues. Information ranges from entertaining and business protocol to the role of interpreters and gift giving.

The U.S. Department of Commerce provides a range of services and publications which can be useful, both to faculty and students. Similarly, Foreign Affairs and International Trade Canada provide information that can be used for this course. Newspapers and business magazines are also helpful in complementing text materials. Regular reading from these sources ensures that students are up-to-date on world events. It is important, therefore, to relate real-world events to class materials. We suggest the following newspapers and magazines:

The Economist   The Wall Street Journal
The Financial Times   The Financial Post
The Globe and Mail Report on Business

Fortune   Business Week
Far East Economic Review

4. Guest Lectures and On-Site Visits:

It is often surprising to professors to find that businesses are not only willing, but often interested, in providing a lecture by one of their executives or an on-site visit. Of course, one has to be sensitive to their needs and be willing to accommodate their time frames, format, etc. This is why arranging these lectures/visits can be quite time consuming. It is often a good idea to begin by identifying organizations which consider themselves friends of the college or university or the business department. These are often friends because of their financial support or they are alumni. Among these organizations there will usually be at least some which are involved in international business. If there are no friends which appear to be particularly appropriate, then broaden the search to all organizations in the community with international activities. Based on the activities of the targeted organization, you can decide whether a guest lecture or an on-site visit would be more appropriate. You can then approach the organization. The approach can be through a personal contact (i.e. someone you or an other faculty member knows personally) or through the Public Relations Department or the International Division. It may be necessary to approach several organizations to find one that fits your needs and schedule.

In addition to business executives as guest lecturers, consider other faculty members, both in the Business Department and throughout the College and University. You will find many people on campus who have lived and worked in foreign locations or for international organizations. They can provide valuable real-life information for students. Many people consider it a compliment to be asked to guest lecture, so do not be cautious about asking. Remember, however, that you will have to accommodate their schedule and this may take some time to organize.

5. Computer Software:

There has been a burgeoning of computer software available for college and university courses. A number of these may be appropriate for your international business course. There are frequent changes and introductions to computer software, so we suggest that you speak to your computer centre for suggestions. Standard & Poor's Compustat Services Inc. has a number of international data bases and programs which may be of interest.

Part IV: General Suggestions for Using Chapter Materials

Each chapter contains a variety of materials that can be used to stimulate class discussions and relate real-world events to topics covered in the chapter. The discussion questions are intended primarily for in-class discussion but some require some outside preparation. They cannot all be covered, therefore the professor or students must select those to be used. Some approaches which are possible are:

(a) A professor can select appropriate discussion questions and be prepared to lead such a discussion.

(b) Students can be assigned to small groups to discuss different questions and be prepared to synthesize their discussion for class.

(c) A professor can select the discussion questions that seem most meaningful for a particular class and assign individuals or groups to prepare them for class presentation and to hand in.

(d) Students can be asked to select discussion questions to prepare for class presentation and discussion.

(e) Discussion questions can also be used as essay questions on tests and examinations.

The chapter by chapter discussion which follows includes some comments on the specific material which is included in each chapter. Our comments on each chapter are brief. We present a summary of the chapter and a suggested class agenda which should be helpful in covering various topics. The discussion questions are self-explanatory, and, depending on how they are used, professors will have different expectations regarding the depth of analysis which students should undertake. Our comments pertain primarily to the in-class discussion. The chapter by chapter discussion is concluded with a test bank of questions for that chapter. This test bank includes multiple choice, true or false, and short essay type questions.

In addition to following the flow of ideas in the text, consider the following ideas for the beginning of the term:

(i) Have students choose a country that they would like to visit as a manger; allow students a week or two to make the decision then have them hand in a brief (one page) description of their chosen country. Students can then consider their chosen country relative to each topic covered during the semester. At the end of the semester, students are asked to reconsider their original decision and explain if and why their decision has changed. Students can also use this country to complete other projects.

(ii) Have students describe, in their own terms, the characteristics important to businesses in the "home" country (Canada or the United States for most students, but foreign students should choose their home country). Ask students to update these characteristics weekly throughout the term relative to the topics covered in each chapter. This "diary" can be handed in at the end of the term.

Chapter 1

Global Management: An Overview

Chapter Summary:

This chapter provides an historical overview of international business as well as thoughts about the future. It stresses that international business is not a new phenomenon but focuses on developments in the twentieth century as of most relevance to students. A number of issues are discussed as likely to be important to international business in the future. Exhibit 1.3 relates to the 'actors' in the international business environment and is particularly useful in drawing students' attention to the variety of international management activities. The increasing complexity of the international business environment can be discussed and students asked to identify "actors" in the current environment, and illustrate their interactions with international businesses.

Suggested Class Agenda:

The purpose of this class is to set global management in an historic context. The first part of the lecture should center around a historical discussion of the global management environment. Students should be encouraged to use their own knowledge of world history to complement this lecture on commercial history. This section of the lecture should also include a review of the actors in the International Management Play. This review should be incorporated into the natural flow of the lecture on global commercial history.

Students should be asked prior to class to complete Discussion Question #3 for this part of the lecture. This section discusses the recent developments in the global management environment. As the lecture progresses, the professor can integrate the student's answers for Question #3 into the integrative discussion.

Overheads:

#1. History of the Global Management Environment

         1500 to 1850: The Commercial Era
         1850 to 1945: The Explorative/Concessionary Era
         1945 to 1970: The National Era
         1970 to 1990: The Turbulent Era

#2 Actors in the International Management Play

         Exhibit #1.3, Page 14.

#3 Recent Developments

         Exhibit #1.4, Page 19.

Discussion Questions:

1.   Review your local newspaper for the past week and select a local story that has been featured during that period. Suppose you were a foreign investor considering investment in your local area, discuss how this news would influence your perception of the attractiveness of the local environment.

     (Answers vary according to the news and the local area)

2.   Select a local store for investigation. Examine a variety of items in their store and identify their country of origin. Discuss the implications of your findings for managers at this store.

     (Answers vary according to the items)

3. Identify a major international event that has occurred in the past six months. Discuss how this is likely to influence managers considering doing business abroad.

   (Once again answers vary)

   {It should be noted that all three discussion questions are intended to focus the students' attention on current events. Students should be encouraged to be innovative. All three questions ask students to put themselves in the position of managers to consider these events. It is often helpful to students to attempt some sort of role playing in order to think about the practical impact of current events on doing business.}

Test Questions:

A: Multiple Choice Questions

1. The discovery of the New World was encouraged by:

   (a) Europe's interest in trade with the Far East (Pg 7)
   (b) a need to find new sources of labour
   (c) expectations of great sources of wealth in the Americas
   (d) explorers who wanted to take advantage of the slave trade

2. According to the text, during which time period was international business first conducted:

   (a) the early 1900's
   (b) the Roman Empire
   (c) the Middle Ages
   (d) the Egyptian Empire (Pg 6)

3. In the 1700's, merchants trading internationally were:

   (a) disliked by their countrymen
   (b) seen as agents of a progressive liberal revolution (Pg 8)
   (c) thought to be exploiting the less fortunate
   (d) expected to investigate investment opportunities for their firms

4. Initially, what was the major reason for American companies becoming international:

   (a) to improve opportunities for executives
   (b) to take advantage of low labour costs in developing countries
   (c) to overcome trade barriers (Pg 8)
   (d) all of the above

5. What is the time period for the Commercial Era of international business evolution:

   (a) 1850 - 1914
   (b) 1500 - 1850 (Pg 8)
   (c) 1945 - 1970
   (d) 1914 - 1945

6. The **XXXX** Era of international business was characterized by industrial empires:

    (a) Commercial
    (b) Explorative   (Pg 9)
    (c) Concessionary
    (d) National
    (e) none of the above

7. The first foreign branch of an American company was located in Scotland. The company was:

    (a) the Hudson's Bay Company
    (b) the Singer Sewing Machine Company   (Pg 8)
    (c) the Remington Rifle Company
    (d) the Revereware Company
    (e) none of the above

8. The Explorative Era was characterized by industrial empires based upon:

    (a) industrial products   (Pg 9)
    (b) precious metals
    (c) spices and silk
    (d) exotic materials

9. The Great Depression of the 1930's encouraged international companies to:

    (a) increase the use of locals in foreign subsidiaries
    (b) to cut back on services that had previously been offered in host countries
    (c) to accept business people in foreign locations seeking greater independence
    (d) a, b & c   (Pg 11)
    (e) none of the above

10. MNC's, as we think of them today, were established during:

    (a) the Commercial Era
    (b) the 1870's
    (c) the Concessionary Era
    (d) the 1950's & 1960's   (Pg 11)

11. Internationalization by U.S. companies suffered a setback in the 1970's because they:

    (a) expanded too quickly
    (b) were successful but culturally insensitive   (Pg 13)
    (c) found their executives `went native' when transferred
    (d) were internationally unsuccessful

12. In the three actor phase of the international business play, who are the three main parties?

    (a) the firm, its commercial constituencies, and the host government   (Pg 15)
    (b) the United States, Europe, and Japan
    (c) the United States, Newly Industrialized Nations, and the Communist countries
    (d) none of the above

13. The four actor stage of international business is increasingly complex because of:

    (a) the concern of interest groups with the activities of international firms
    (b) the concern to the UNCTNC with the activities of international firms
    (c) the concern of the home government with the activities of their firms in foreign locations (Pg 16)
    (d) the concern of the host government with activities of foreign firms in the host country

14. Considering current trends and what they may mean for the future of international business is:

    (a) like Yogi Berra predicting the future of baseball
    (b) worthwhile as a guide to making decisions about the future   (Pg 18)
    (c) risky, and generally left to fortune tellers and soothsayers
    (d) not likely to provide helpful information for international companies

15. A successful MNC has to be **XXX** and **YYY**, in order to function effectively in today's uncertain and complex environment:

    (a) conservative and cautious
    (b) flexible and adaptable   (Pg 23)
    (c) concerned with traditional practices and functional structures
    (d) none of the above

B: True or False Questions

F **(Pg 7)**   1. The early Olympic games served as a meeting place for people from many locations but commercial activities were not allowed during the Games.

T **(Pg 6)**   2. The European discovery of North America can be partly attributed to the European desire for spices and exotic goods.

F **(Pg 11)**   3. The National Era (1945-1970) of international business was characterized by decreasing hostility toward Western enterprises.

T **(Pg 10)**   4. The Concessionary Era (1914-1945) of international business was characterized by an increasing paternalism of Western enterprises in foreign locations.

F **(Pg 11)**   5. The National Era of international business was one of increased stability because of the independence of many former colonies.

T **(Pg 13)**   6. During the 1970's, the Japanese became increasingly successful in their internationalization of business.

F **(Pg 18)**   7. **The Futurist** argues that mid-sized operations are growing because current market conditions favour these companies.

T **(Pg 20)**   8. According to Jim MacNeil, environmental issues have recently been forces to the top political agendas in all the major capitals of the world.

F **(Pg 21)**   9. International firms have sought the advice of the UNCTNC because outside regulation is easier to comply with than self-regulation.

T **(Pg 22)**   10. The differences between capitalism and communism have had a major impact on business in the twentieth century.

C: Short Essay Questions

1. Identify and discuss the major changes which occurred in international business 1500 to 1945.

(Pgs 6-11)

2. Identify and discuss the actors identified in the text as participating in each of the four stages of international business development.

(Pgs 13-17)

3. Select one of the events identified in the text as influencing international business in coming years and discuss how this event might influence international firms.

(Pgs 17-23)

Chapter 2

Global Management in the Context of Politics

Chapter Summary:

Political systems are inextricably tied into the existence of national boundaries. This chapter considers the political environment as one of importance to all companies with international activities. Differing relationships of government and business and the risks inherent in dealing with governments are examined. A major focus of the chapter is defining and discussing political risk and ways of managing this risk. The chapter emphasizes the idea that political risk is a function of both country characteristics and company characteristics, and that it must be assessed and managed in this context. The characteristics associated with country risk and company risk are summarized under the section on Vulnerability to Risk. This section is particularly useful for discussing these issues. Similarly, the sections dealing with defensive and integrative political risk management techniques provide helpful summaries. It is important to stress that while these techniques are discussed as contrasting choices, most firms will use a combination of the two.

Suggested Class Agenda:

The focus of this lecture will be the political risk assessment. In order to facilitate this discussion the lecture will be constructed around the Political Risk Management Process developed by Gregory (1989) found on page 53. To begin the lecture it would be helpful to briefly review the major types of governments. This then leads into a discussion of corporate-government relationships. The section of the lecture should introduce the students to the issue of relating to host governments. This should include both the views of the MNC and the host government itself. The next section of the lecture will then flow to the types of political risk which companies face. The three categories (forced divestment, unwelcome regulation, and interference with operations) will be discussed using examples.

The bulk of the lecture will begin after the above material has been covered. This next section will focus on the Political Risk Management Process developed by Gregory (1989) found on page 53. Going through the model step by step the professor will be able to incorporate much of the chapter material. Much of the model is self explanatory, but there are two steps which can be expanded for discussion. Starting at **Step 1**, the discussion should turn to company and country characteristics which influence the amount of risk faced by a company.

The other step is **Step 3**, when the corporation selects management techniques to deal with risk. The professor should incorporate Gregory's approaches to managing political risk: **defensive** and **integrative**.

Overheads:

#1. Types of Governments

> *Capitalist*
> *Socialist*
> *Communist*

#2. Relating to Host Governments

> *MNC View*   *all things good (Pgs 37-39)*
>
> *Host View*   *all things bad   (Pgs 39-42)*
>
> *Mixed View*   *Exhibit #2.1   (Pg 43)*

#3 Categories of Political Risk

> *Forced Divestment*
> *Unwelcome Regulation*
> *Interference with Operations*

#4 Political Risk Management Process

> *Step 1: Identify Risks*
> *Step 2: Evaluate Risks*
> *Step 3: Select Management Techniques*
> *Step 4: Implement Techniques*
> *Step 5: Evaluate Success*

#5   Step 1: Identify Risks

Country Characteristics
> *Type of government*
> *Level of economic development*
> *Stability of social systems*
> *Stability of political systems*

Company Characteristics
> *Industry*
> *Technology*
> *Ownership*
> *Management*

#6   Step 3: Select Management Techniques

Defensive Approaches to Political Risk Management
> *Financial techniques*
> *Managerial techniques*
> *Logistical techniques*
> *Marketing techniques*

Integrative Approaches to Political Risk Management
> *Managerial techniques*
> *Government Relations techniques*
> *Financial techniques*

Discussion Questions:

1.   *"Ethnic differences are often a major component of political risk."* Discuss this statement, giving recent examples to illustrate.

      (Pgs 45-50 for the over-all discussion)

2.   Political parties have traditionally been defined on a spectrum of "left" or "right." Describe what is meant by each of these terms and discuss how parties at the extreme of the spectrum generally view the role of business in society.

      (Definitions = Pgs 34-35
      Discussion   = Pgs 35-36)

3.   Using your local community as an example, identify the attitudes of local residents towards foreign investment (use local media stores, discussions with students and friends, interviews with local business managers). Discuss how the attitudes you have identified influence the degree of political risk associated with investment in you community.

      (Answers will vary, but all should include a discussion from Pgs 45-50)

Test Questions:

A: Multiple Choice Questions

1. Which of the following types of political risk is most difficult to assess and manage:

   (a) interference with operations   (Pgs 45-47)
   (b) forced divestment
   (c) unwelcome regulations
   (d) all of the above are equally difficult

2. Forced divestment, unwelcome regulation and interference with operations are consequences of:

   (a) political risk   (Pgs 45-47)
   (b) negotiations with unions
   (c) international trade regulation
   (d) advanced government policies

3. When forced divestment occurs, which of the following is/are most likely:

   (a) payment for assets is less than the company considers equitable
   (b) payment is in non-convertible currency
   (c) the loss of a foreign subsidiary affects the rest of the organization's operations
   (d) all the company assets are confiscated by the host company
   (e) all of the above
   (f) a, b & c   (Pg 46)

4. Unwelcome regulations imposed on foreign firms by a host government are likely to include all of the following procedures, <u>except</u>:

   (a) extra corporate income tax
   (b) local ownership requirements
   (c) restrictions on reinvestment and repatriation of profits
   (d) restrictions on personnel transfers to head office   (Pg 46)

5. Discriminatory government support of locally owned and operated businesses falls into which category of political risk?

  (a) forced divestment
  (b) unwelcome regulations
  (c) interference with operations   (Pg 47)
  (d) none of the above

6. Which kind of political risk is most difficult to assess and manage because of its serious subtle forms and less obvious immediate effects?

  (a) forced divestment
  (b) unwelcome regulations
  (c) interference with operations   (Pg 47)
  (d) all of the above are equally difficult

7. The information needed to assess political risk comes from external and internal sources. An external source would be:

  (a) staff personnel
  (b) regional managers
  (c) banks
  (d) accounting firms
  (e) all of the above
  (f) a & b
  (g) c & d   (Pg 51)

8. According to Gregory, evaluating political risk consists of the following:

  (a) identify risks, evaluate risk, select management techniques, evaluate success (Pg 53)
  (b) select management techniques, apply it to risks, evaluate success
  (c) evaluate risks, select management techniques, evaluate success
  (d) none of the above

9. The degree of risk faced by a company is a function of:

    (a) the host country and its political structure
    (b) the size of the company and investment size
    (c) government, economic and social instability
    (d) both the particular country and the particular company's operations   (Pg 53)

10. Which of the following country characteristics would affect the degree of political risk:

    (a) type of government
    (b) level of economic development
    (c) stability of social and political systems
    (d) a & c
    (e) all of the above   (Pg 48)

11. Which of the following foreign investments would be most subject to political risk:

    (a) a small bank   (Pgs 49-50)
    (b) a small, high-tech manufacturer
    (c) a medium sized key punch operation
    (d) a joint-venture with a local private partner in the tourist industry
    (e) they would be equally subject to risk

12. Which of the following companies would be <u>least</u> likely to suffer from host government intervention in its operations:

    (a) a wholly owned, low-tech production subsidiary
    (b) a joint-venture with the government in the mining business
    (c) a medium sized, high-tech joint venture with local partners   (Pgs 49-50)
    (d) a small, foreign managed assembly plant

13. What type of business is relatively safe in terms of its protection against political risk?

    (a) a bank
    (b) a company involved in infrastructure projects
    (c) a company extracting natural resources from the host country
    (d) a high-tech company   (Pg 49)

14. Generally speaking, all of the following foreign investments are relatively safe from the intervention of host government, <u>except</u>:

   (a) an R&D-extensive company
   (b) a company with great competitive edge
   (c) an insurance company   (Pgs 49-50)
   (d) a high-tech company

15. Which of the following is <u>not</u> a company characteristic that influences the level of political risk:

   (a) type of industry and operations
   (b) form of ownership
   (c) nationality of management
   **(d) degree to which a foreign subsidiary retains profits in host country
         (Pgs 49-50)**

16. Which of the following are relatively safe from government interference:

   (a) companies with relatively low R&D expenditure
   (b) companies with complex, globally integrated operations   (Pgs 49-50)
   (c) companies with many competitors
   (d) none of the above

17. Which of the following are types of companies or industries that are relatively safe from government intervention:

   (a) companies with complex, globally integrated operations
   (b) high-tech companies with high R&D expenditures
   (c) companies with little competition
   (d) all of the above   (Pgs 49-50)

18. The two basic approaches to managing political risk are:

    (a) dependence and integration
    (b) offensive and defensive
    (c) offensive and integrative
    (d) **defensive and integrative**   **(Pg 55)**

19. Defensive political risk management techniques include the following:

    (a) hiring locals at all levels in the organization
    (b) increasing communication with local government'
    (c) **controlling markets outside of the host country**   **(Pgs 55-56)**
    (d) a & b
    (e) all of the above

20. All of following approaches are considered as defensive political risk management strategies, <u>except</u>:

    (a) **concentration of R&D in host country**   **(Pgs 55-56)**
    (b) raising capital from a variety of sources
    (c) minimizing the use of host nationals in strategic positions
    (d) controlling supply sources for the operation

21. Defensive approaches to political risk management would <u>not</u> include:

    (a) raising capital from host countries
    (b) minimizing locals in strategic positions
    (c) **transferring workers from parent company**   **(Pgs 55-56)**
    (d) concentrating R&D in home country

22. A defensive approach to managing political risk means:

    (a) making the firm an integral part of host society
    (b) **reducing dependence on any single subsidiary**   **(Pgs 55-56)**
    (c) entering a joint venture agreement with a local company
    (d) 100% ownership

23. Which of the following would be considered an integrative approach to managing political risk:

    (a)   sourcing from multiple locations
    (b)   selling a substantial portion of a subsidiary's shares on the local (host) stock exchange (Pgs 57-58)
    (c)   carrying out R&D in the parent company
    (d)   all of the above are integrative approaches

24. Managing political risk through integrative techniques might include:

    (a)   increasing local ownership and sourcing   (Pgs 57-58)
    (b)   maintaining control of external markets and supplies
    (c)   a globally integrated production system
    (d)   centralized financial decisions

25. All of the following techniques are considered as integrative strategies of political risk management, <u>except</u>:

    (a)   establishing commitment to the company among local employees
    (b)   entering into a joint venture with firms from third countries   (Pgs 57-58)
    (c)   providing public services, such as education, health and transportation
    (d)   raising equity in the host country

26. From the MNC's viewpoint, it can bring benefits to the host government in terms of:

        (i)   capital for growth and development
        (ii)   technologies for modernization
        (iii) skills for local industries
        (iv) access to foreign markets

    (a)   ii, iii & iv
    (b)   ii & iii
    (c)   i, ii & iii
    (d)   i, ii, iii & iv   (Pgs 36-39)

27. Which of the following would provide for a strong host country position in dealing with an MNC?

    (a)   **many other MNC's available to country**   **(Pg 43)**
    (b)   no other company has technology needed by country
    (c)   many companies available, technology widely known
    (d)   host country has trade barriers for MNC product

28. The bargaining posture of an MNC and a host government are most likely to be quiet and unobtrusive and aim for little interaction when:

    (a)   both sides are strong
    (b)   relative strength is unclear
    (c)   **both sides are weak**   **(Pg 43)**
    (d)   none of the above

29. A country where the government owns the basic means of production combined with private ownership of other factors would have a **XXXX** government.

    (a)   capitalist
    (b)   socialist
    (c)   **communist**   **(Pg 35)**
    (d)   fascist

30. Risk <u>cannot</u> be:

    (a)   reduced
    (b)   transferred
    (c)   **eliminated**   **(Throughout Chapter)**
    (d)   avoided
    (e)   all of the above apply to risk

B: True of False Questions

F   <u>(Pg 46)</u>   1. The risk of unwanted takeovers increased through the 1980's.

F   <u>(Pg 45)</u>   2. Under international law, a forced divestment is illegal even with a prompt and equitable compensation.

T   <u>(Pg 46)</u>   3. In a particular country there are well-known and relatively stable regulations concerning foreign firms; even if these regulations make foreign operations less profitable, we cannot say that foreign firms are exposed to political risk.

T   <u>(Pg 47)</u>   4. Political risk that involves government activities including subtle discrimination against foreign businesses is often particularly difficult to manage.

T   <u>(Pg 50)</u>   5. Political risk strategies continue to rely largely on subjective judgements, although risk assessment is increasingly being formalized by international companies.

T   <u>(Pg 48)</u>   6. Management usually believes that the stability of a government is more important than whether a nation is a democracy or a dictatorship.

F   <u>(Pg 48)</u>   7. Because acts of terrorism are rare, international firms ignore them.

F   <u>(Pg 49)</u>   8. Local ownership is usually viewed favourably by host governments; therefore, a joint-venture with a host government is relatively low in political risk.

T   <u>(Pg 50)</u>   9. Although host governments usually favour local composition of management, the government is likely to intervene in a foreign company whose management team is 100% local.

F   <u>(Pg 50)</u>   10. A large company is vulnerable to political risk because take over by a host government can result in great political visibility among locals; therefore, the smaller foreign firm is safer.

T   <u>(Pg 55)</u>   11. Maximizing debt investment would be classified as a defensive financial approach to political risk management.

F　　**(Pg 58)**　　　　12.　Since the integrative and defensive strategies of political risk management are two dramatically different approaches, an MNC should choose one of them and will find it very difficult to combine these two approaches.

C: Short Essay Questions

1. Define political risk and discuss the main categories of political risk identified in the text.
(Pgs 49-50)

2. Identify and discuss the main integrative techniques that are used to manage political risk.
(Pgs 57-58)

3. Identify and discuss the main defensive techniques that are used to manage political risk.
(Pgs 55-56)

4. Identify three company characteristics that influence the level of political risk to which a company is exposed and discuss how these affect the political risk environment.
(Pgs 47-50)

Chapter 3

The Cultural Environment

Chapter Summary:

This chapter is intended to emphasize the need to be sensitive to cultural differences in international business activities. A number of approaches to cultural differences are explored and related to doing business, and managing, internationally. Any discussion of cultural values in a particular society, and cultural differences between societies, is, in effect, cultural stereotyping. This needs to be stressed to students and the cultural stereotyping explained as a description of the average preference in any society which still allows for a wide degree of individual variation within each society.

This can be illustrated as follows:

> ** *People in both Canada and the United States are generally considered individualistic; nevertheless, some people are more group-oriented than this norm would suggest.*

> ** *People in Japan are generally considered to be group-oriented; nevertheless, some Japanese are as individualistic as their Canadian and American counterparts.*

It is also important to emphasize that one set of cultural values is in no way "right" and another "wrong".

Suggested Class Agenda:

This lecture should begin with a discussion of **"What is Culture?"** This should include the definition on page 70 and discussion of several of the elements of this definition. This section of the lecture will also include an introduction to **"How we study culture."** This introduction will serve as the basis of the rest of the lecture.

The professor may begin by saying that the best way to understand how another culture differs from this home culture is to start by gaining an understanding of the home culture. The subsequent discussion of what the "home culture" is should be directed by the students in an interactive discussion.

Next the lecture should segue into a more in-depth presentation of what is culture. The model developed by Punnett and found on page 78 will form an centre point for this discussion. The seven parameters of the model should be covered and their interaction can be a starting point for debate.

Finally, the lecture should cover how an organization conducts a "cultural assessment". The six factors discussed in the text (language, religion, education, social systems, level of development, and nation/culture) provide a generous amount of material for class discussion. This discussion will be enhanced if students are encouraged to discuss their own cultures.

Overheads:

#1 "What is Culture"

> *"Culture is a learned, shared, compelling, interrelated set of symbols whose meaning provides a set of orientations for members of a society. These orientations, taken together, provide solutions to problems that all societies must solve if they are to remain viable."*

> * Learned
> * Shared
> * Compelling
> * Interrelated
> * Provides Orientation to People

#2   Cultural Underpinnings

   Exhibit #3.1   (Page 78)

   1. National Variables
   2. Societal Variables
   3. Societal/National Culture
   4. Corporate Culture
   5. Professional Culture
   6. Individual Values
   7. Behaviour

#3 Assessing Cultural Factors

   1. Language
   2. Religion
   3. Education
   4. Social Systems
   5. Level of Development
   6. Nation or Culture

#4   Language

   Exhibit #3.2   (Page 83)

#5 Religion

   Exhibit #3.3   (Pages 86-87)

#6 The World's Most Common Religions

   * *Hinduism*
   * *Buddhism*
   * *Islam*
   * *Christianity*

#7 Education

> * *Staffing Policies*
> * *Training*
> * *Level of Decentralization*

#8 Social Systems

> * *Courting and Marriage Rituals*
> * *Entertaining Practices*
> * *Interaction of "Classes"*
> * *Kinship Units*
> * *Business Ownership*

#9 Level of Development

> 1. *Third World*
> 2. *Less Developed Countries (LDC)*
> 3. *Developing Countries*
> 4. *Newly Industrializing Countries (NIC)*
> 5. *Centrally Planned Economies*
> 6. *Developed/Industrialized Countries*

Discussion Questions:

1. Using your local community as an example, describe its cultural characteristics. Discuss the degree of cultural homogeneity or diversity found in your community. How does this homogeneity or diversity affect foreign managers coming to your community.

    (This is usually most effective before discussing the content of the chapter. The main idea is to get students to discuss their own interpretation of the concepts and their impact, rather than reiterating the ideas in the chapter. Culture is a subjective concept and therefore students should be encouraged to express their own ideas.)

2. Develop a cultural profile of your home country to be provided to foreign managers working in the home country.

    (Identifying and understanding your own culture is difficult, but particularly valuable because it forces self-examination. The exercise posed here can be used to begin this self-examination. Students can be asked to respond to this issue, and given ten to fifteen minutes to think about it and write their responses. A general discussion of what it means to be "Canadian", "American" or any other culture can then be based on these notes.)

3. Select two countries that you believe be to quite different culturally. Identify the cultural differences between these two countries and discuss how the differences identified are likely to influence interactions between managers from these two countries.

    (Answers will vary but should include a discussion of the material from Pages 79 to 103)

Test Questions:

A: Multiple Choice

1. Culture can be defined in many ways, but important components seem to be:

    (a) culture is learned and shared by a group
    (b) culture is an inter-relationship of factors
    (c) culture is a guide to acceptable attitudes and behaviour
    (d) culture is both continuous and changing
    (e) all of the above   (Pgs 70-72)

2. Which of the following is <u>not</u> considered true of culture:

    (a) culture is shared
    (b) culture directs behaviour
    (c) culture is inherited   (Pgs 70-72)
    (d) culture consists of interrelated characteristics

3. MNCs are interested in national cultures for which of the following reasons:

    (a) labour mobility leads to a national workforce   (Pg 102)
    (b) it is almost inevitable that there will be a variety of sub-cultures in any nation
    (c) the same culture may well be found in several different countries
    (d) cultural differences are difficult to assess and understand
    (e) all of the above

4. Which of the following statement is correct:

    (a) one culture can exist in more than one nation
    (b) one country can encompass more than one culture
    (c) from an MNC's point of view, cultural analysis begins with the national culture
    (d) a & b
    (e) a, b & c   (Pgs 101-103)

5. Based on the discussion in the text, all of the following factors are considered national variables, <u>except</u>:

    (a) laws and regulations
    (b) religion   (Pg 77)
    (c) economic conditions
    (d) political ideology

6. Which of the following influence the development of individual values:

    (a) language and religion
    (b) national laws
    (c) social customs
    (d) all of the above   (Pgs 77-79)
    (e) a & c

7. <u>**XXXX**</u> defines and perpetuates a particular world view.

    (a) ethnocentrism
    (b) language   (Pg 80)
    (c) culture
    (d) a country's laws

8. When one language is translated into another, and then translated back and examined to see if there are any discrepancies, this process is called:

    (a) straight translation
    (b) translation/back translation   (Pg 82)
    (c) translation/counter translation
    (d) double translation

9. Religion is an important aspect of a nation's culture and influences the operation of an international company because:

    (a) religion can influence many daily activities of foreign firm
    (b) the importance of religion in a particular society can be a major consideration in setting up policies and procedures
    (c) different beliefs among different religious sects can usually be overcome easily
    (d) all of the above
    (e) a & b   (Pg 85)

10. The educational system and educational attainment in a country will affect an MNC's operations by influencing:

   (a) the staffing policy
   (b) the design of employee training programs
   (c) type of communication used
   (d) all of the above   (Pg 92)
   (e) a & b

11. The educational system and educational attainment in a particular country will have an impact on communication in an international company, especially communication between a subsidiary and:

   (a) its parent company in the home country
   (b) its employees   (Pg 92)
   (c) the host government
   (d) its suppliers

B: True or False Questions

F   **(Pg 70)**   1. Culture is innate, not learned.

F   **(Pg 75)**   2. Since culture is composed of a variety of aspects (i.e. language, religion, education, etc.), people are easily aware of the influence of the culture in their daily life.

F   **(Pg 101)**   3. The existence of culture coincides with a country's national boundaries.

T   **(Pg 102)**   4. Although there may be different cultures in a particular country, the MNC would usually emphasize the national culture in a cultural analysis.

F   <u>(Pg 88)</u>   5. It is difficult for an MNC to understand a foreign country's religion because there is very little literature available on the beliefs and practices of religions in other parts of the world.

F   <u>(Pg 91)</u>   6. Education is regarded as one aspect of a nations culture, but, unlike language and religion, this factor rarely has much impact on an MNC's decisions.

T   <u>(Pg 92)</u>   7. A training program for a bank in Japan might incorporate Zen meditation and military training.

F   <u>(Pg none)</u>   8. A training program for a bank in India would likely incorporate tsi chi meditation and Uzi training.

C: Short Essay Questions

1. Based on the text's definition of culture, identify the main characteristics of culture and discuss their implications for international business.

<u>(Definition = Pgs 70-72)</u>
<u>(Implications = Pgs 70-72)</u>

2. Some cultures transcend national borders and some countries have many cultures within their boundaries. Explain why, from an international firm's point of view, the main concern is the national culture. Address your explanation to the perspective of the human resource management team.

<u>(Pg 102)</u>

Chapter 4

International Labor Relations

Chapter Summary:

Technological advances notwithstanding, people still make up organizations. Relations with "labor" need to be cultivated and managed, and this is complex in a global environment. When multiple cultures and social norms collide, labor management practices become a very complicated matter indeed. This chapter provides a review of key labor relations terminology, and proceeds to discuss labor practices of MNCs. The problems/nuances of cross-national labor management are illustrated by a comparative analysis of several countries, in particular the US, Italy, and Britain. Important trends in labor relations round up the chapter, and offer a useful discussion point for students, who may be asked to look at the literature and find illustrative examples to highlight/add to the trends identified in the text.

Suggested Agenda:

Prior to this class, students may be asked to do some library (even primary!) research to facilitate discussion of (a) comparative labor relations practices in countries other than the three identified in the chapter, and (b) trends in labor relations, especially in the area of quality control.

The beginning of the session would benefit from a quick overview of labor relations terminology, and a brief lecture on the diverse labor environment facing the MNC. This could be followed by an interactive discussion, possibly led by the students, on the two topics suggested above.

The discussion questions at the end of the chapter provide a logical pause and conclusion to the session.

Overheads:

Recommend ONE overhead. Use Deming's 14 points on Quality, re: Pgs 124-125.

Discussion Questions:

1. Select two countries and discuss contrasts in their approaches to labor relations.

    (refer to Pgs 113-116 for examples. Other countries of special interest may include Canada, Japan, and Germany)

2. Identify evidence of cultural diversity in your local workforce. Discuss how this diversity is likely to affect management approaches.

    (reference Pg 116, and Pgs 120-122 for ideas)

3. Has the internationalization of the labor union movement kept pace with the internationalization of business? Discuss.

    Essentially no. (refer to Pgs 119-120 for more detail)

Test Questions:

A. Multiple Choice

1.   Collective bargaining refers to:

     (a)   a buyers group negotiating a product's price with the supplier.
     (b)   **a process of negotiation to formalize a labor contract.**   **(Pg 110)**
     (c)   a cultural barrier because people are different.
     (d)   a church collecting donations from its parishioners.

2.   A strike or a lockout is expensive for management because:

     (a)   the company continues to incur overhead costs.
     (b)   production stops so units are not manufactured.
     (c)   the firm's market share may suffer.
     (d)   **all of the above.**   **(Pg 111)**

3.   A strike or a lockout is expensive for labor because:

     (a)   **striking or locked-out workers may face economic hardship.**   **(Pg 111)**
     (b)   picket signs cost a lot of money to make.
     (c)   the company confiscates the workers' belongings left on premises.
     (d)   union members illegally can only strike three times.

4.   The main difference between a mediator and an arbitrator is that:

     (a)   an arbitrator costs a lot of money.
     (b)   mediators are only used in international settings.
     (c)   arbitrators are appointed by the government.
     (d)   **an arbitrator's decisions are binding.**   **(Pg 112)**

5.   In the US, labor negotiations are usually viewed in financial terms. In Europe, they are often seen as:

     (a)   **a class struggle.**   **(Pg 112)**
     (b)   a friendly chat.
     (c)   a cultural exchange.
     (d)   a negotiating-skills training.

6.   Union membership in the US:

       (a)   is on the rise and has exceeded 95% participation.
       (b)   is required by federal law.
       (c)   **is half of what it was in 1955.**   **(Pg 114)**
       (d)   is much higher than most other developed nations.

7.   Transnational sourcing is a strategy often employed by MNCs to:

       (a)   ignore the laws of host countries.
       (b)   **rely on their foreign subsidiaries as a source of components. (Pg 117)**
       (c)   extract natural resources from other countries.
       (d)   transfer their staff from one nation to another.

8.   Dual sourcing strategies make companies less vulnerable to strikes at any single subsidiary, but:

       (a)   are illegal in most countries.
       (b)   dual sources are impossible to locate in reality.
       (c)   **the efficiency of the MNC may be impaired.**   **(Pg 117)**
       (d)   US anti-trust laws prohibit dual sourcing.

9.   MNCs may wish to decentralize labor relations management to foreign subsidiaries especially if:

       (a)   **cultural subtleties and local practices are expected to be important elements in that environment.**   **(Pg 118)**
       (b)   their competitors are doing just that.
       (c)   local subsidiary management expresses a desire to take over the role.
       (d)   the two countries (head office and subsidiary) are highly similar.

10.   International Trade Secretariats (ITS) are:

       (a)   trade tribunals set up to arbitrate international trade disputes.
       (b)   manufacturers' associations aimed at promoting trade.
       (c)   **labor unions' response to the MNC challenge internationally. (Pg 119)**
       (d)   trade cabals set up by MNCs to exploit Third World countries.

11.   The QC circle is:

(a)   a quality control process based on the work on W. E. Deming. (Pg 123)
(b)   a circular process that controls quality of output by making the first worker in the assembly line responsible for all defects.
(c)   only workable in Japan because it is unique to their culture.
(d)   a roundtable of randomly selected workers to discuss labor practices.

12.   Quality control, according to Deming, has to do with:

(a)   instilling fear among workers, so that they are afraid to make a mistake.
(b)   a regiment of mass inspections to ensure good quality.
(c)   increasing the number of vendors so as to minimize over-reliance on any one source.
(d)   none of the above.   (Pgs124-125)

13.   Middle managers often are cynical towards quality circle and similar quality improving ideas because:

(a)   these concepts only work in Japan.
(b)   they may fear a loss of power.   (Pg 125)
(c)   they are not concerned with quality control.
(d)   quality circles cost too much money.

14.   Companies may be inclined to share profits with workers because:

(a)   of self-interest, since profit-sharing is a motivational tool.   (Pg 126)
(b)   they do not then have to pay wages to the workers.
(c)   companies are generally becoming more altruistic.
(d)   all of the above.

15.   ESOPs may work if:

(a)   management is strongly committed to it.
(b)   employees are able to contribute to decision making.
(c)   management and employees see their relationship as a partnership.
(d)   all of the above.   (Pg 128)

B. True or False Questions

F (Pg 110)   1. Labor relations encompass only compensation-related issues, and must be governed by a written contract.

T (Pg 111)   2. The way unions represent their members in collective bargaining may vary widely from country to country.

T (Pg 112)   3. Grievances are formal complaints that an employee is not being treated fairly according to the labor agreement.

T (Pg 114)   4. In the US, state laws govern whether or not all workers in a firm must join the union once a union is certified.

F (Pg 116)   5. In Britain, unions seldom strike and union membership is less widespread than in the US.

T (Pg 118)   6. In addition to sourcing issues when setting policy on central oversight of subsidiary labor relations, MNCs must consider environmental and safety questions, public image, and ethical practices.

T (Pg 119)   7. International Trade Secretariats (ITS) have had limited success, and often receive little support from local unions.

F (Pg 120)   8. In the US, labor and management have a trusting relationship and both see the other as a partner. As a result, US MNCs are experts in managing labor relations.

T (Pg 123)   9. The success of quality control strategies such as quality circle and total quality control is dependent upon labor relations, especially management's attitudes towards them.

F (Pg 124)   10. "Quality," according to Deming, means making sure you fix it right every time a customer complains.

C. Short Essay Questions

1.   Why is the number of workers represented by unions considerably lower in the US than in other developed countries?

      (Pgs 113-114)

2.   It has been suggested that transnational firms must keep labor relations central to their strategic planning. Why is that?

      (Pgs 117-118)

3.   Profit Sharing and ESOPs are beginning to see wider adoption worldwide. What are the main reasons why companies may be willing to adopt such strategies? What are some conditions that facilitate the strategy's success?

      (Pgs 126-128)

Chapter 5

The Global Ethical Environment

Chapter Summary:

Virtually every decision an international manager makes involves issues of justice, legality, fairness, equity, right vs. wrong, and human decency. These decisions become increasingly difficult in cross-cultural contexts because of differing beliefs and social customs. At the same time, different societies have developed their own codes of conducts, and some of these ethical codes may be universal among nations while others vary. This chapter discusses the importance of business ethics, both internationally and domestically. Three key concepts-- individual relativism, cultural relativism, and universalism--are introduced to help analyze the realm of international business ethics. Real world problems are used as examples to illustrate the discussion points. For example, bribery as a common practice around the world provides a useful backdrop for a class discussion on ethical standards internationally. Ethical dilemmas faced by managers of MNCs are highlighted, and legal constraints such as the Foreign Corrupt Practices Act are discussed. Suggestions and guidelines are offered to managers in dealing with ethical dilemmas.

Suggested Class Agenda:

For students in the US, it would be useful to provide a brief lecture on the Foreign Corrupt Practices Act and some of its more salient features. In addition, the Civil Rights Act of 1991 and its impact on MNCs should be given some "air time." Such legal constraints are important to the US-based manager, and the class would benefit from a general discussion on their implications.

For students in other countries, it may be useful to bring in additional material pertaining to similar legal constraints as imposed by their governments.

As an in-class exercise, students can be asked (in a previous session) to search the literature for examples of international ethical issues confronting an MNC. In this sessions, some "exemplary" cases can then be used to generate a stimulating class discussion.

If the class benefits from a culturally-diverse group of students, then a sharing of insights in a multicultural/national context would be an educational experience for the participants. In a similar fashion, an experiential exercise can be developed, by asking students from different cultural backgrounds to analyze the ethical issues of the same problem. This should highlight very different perspectives and would serve as a good way for students to reflect on their own cultural biases and "baggage."

Overheads:

#1   What is business ethics?

Business Ethics: The moral principles and standards that guide behavior in the world of business.

#2   Key Concepts in International Business Ethics

Individual Relativism: There is no absolute. The individual decides.

Cultural Relativism: "When in Rome..."

Universalism: "My way or the highway"

Discussion Questions:

1.   Discuss the two main contrasting approaches of ethics presented here; what are your personal reactions to these approaches?

        (see Pgs 141-144)

2.   Review recent newspaper articles and identify one current ethical issue faced by an international company. Discuss and evaluate the company's reactions.

        (answers vary. A good question is why the student considers the issue an ethical one.)

3.   Interview managers in companies in the local community to identify their ethical concerns.

        (answers vary)

Test Questions:

A. Multiple Choice Questions

1.   For the MNC manager, personal values and organizational situational needs sometimes clash in cross-cultural situations, because:

   (a)   managers and employees have differing sociocultural values (Pg 141)
   (b)   they are unfit for the job.
   (c)   they should not personally place a value on organizational needs.
   (d)   a manager undergoes extreme personal changes cross-culturally.

2.   Individual Relativism suggests that:

   (a)   What is ethical is dependent on the individual's cultural background and relative to legal constraints.
   (b)   there is no absolute right or wrong. What is ethical or not depends entirely on the individual. (Pgs 141-142)
   (c)   An individual's actions can be judged relative to what others are doing.
   (d)   Each individual must be ethical or else everything becomes relative.

3.   The idea that what is right or wrong depends on one's culture is called:

   (a)   absolute culturalism.
   (b)   universalism culturalism.
   (c)   relational universalism.
   (d)   cultural relativism. (Pg 142)

4.   Universalists would contend that:

   (a)   everyone should behave ethically so that the world becomes a better place.
   (b)   as long as people universally speak the same language, cultural barriers will break down.
   (c)   if the world is to have any hope of enduring social stability, values will have to be negotiated and universally adopted. (Pg 143)
   (d)   all of the above.

5.   According to the Foreign Corrupt Practices Act, the major distinction between a bribe and an extortion is that:

(a)   **extortions are payments made under duress while bribes are offered voluntarily. (Pg 145)**
(b)   bribe involves money while extortion can be of a non-monetary nature.
(c)   bribes are legal if under $10,000.
(d)   none of the above.

6.   Two things distinguish a "grease payment" from a bribe. One is that the amount involved is small. The other is:

(a)   it is only used by oil companies.
(b)   a receipt must be obtained.
(c)   **it is not designed to seek unlawful competitive advantages. (Pg 146)**
(d)   it is specifically requested by the recipient.

7.   "Agents Fees" are:

(a)   just another name for bribes.
(b)   **fees that a company pays an agent to help them do business in another country. (Pg 146)**
(c)   fees charged by customs agents who help MNCs clear customs when products are being shipped from one country to another.
(d)   salaries paid to managers of overseas subsidiaries, since they are in essence "agents" of the MNC.

8.   Companies can be fined for the illegal actions of their agents if:

(a)   **they have a "reason to know" that part of the fees are used by the agent as bribes. (Pg 146)**
(b)   if the agent is convicted locally.
(c)   the fee exceeds $500,000.
(d)   the agent is a foreign government official.

9.   Social responsibility means:

      (a)   making sure that the company's actions are totally legal.

      (b)   introducing the ethical standards of the US to underdeveloped countries.

      (c)   keeping part of the subsidiary's profits locally.

      (d)   the company has a broader constituency to serve than stockholders. (Pg 149)

10.   The Bhopal incident is a good example of:

      (a)   the consequences of not meeting local laws.

      (b)   the consequences of bribery.

      (c)   the inadequacy of merely meeting local legal requirements. (Pg 150)

      (d)   extortion by Third World governments.

11.   If an MNC pays higher-than-average wages locally,

      (a)   it will always be met with open arms.

      (b)   it still runs the risk of being accused of hoarding the brightest talent from the local talent pool. (Pg 152)

      (c)   it becomes inefficient and will risk subpar performance.

      (d)   it is giving money away.

12.   Promoting local nationals to manage subsidiaries

      (a)   can be seen as creating a "brain drain." (Pg 152)

      (b)   is the best policy for an MNC.

      (c)   is nothing but a public relations gimmick.

      (d)   may not be legal under US law.

13.   The role of "bridge builder" for an expatriate manager means:

      (a)   he/she should help the local community in projects such as bridge-building, so as to improve the logistics of the foreign country.

      (b)   paying close attention to the quality of their relationships with the local communities. (Pg 154)

      (c)   serving as the eyes and ears of one's home country in a foreign land.

      (d)   looking out for major civil construction projects locally so that the MNC can bid on the projects.

14. Compliance with the Civil Rights Act of 1991 may result in MNCs filling overseas positions with more host-national managers *and*

    (a)   **increasing the complexity in the recruitment and selection process for overseas positions. (Pg 156)**
    (b)   paying more in agent fees.
    (c)   hiring only culturall-sensitive individuals.
    (d)   ensuring their candidates are active in promoting civil rights.

15. Well-educated and trained Eastern Europeans are willing to take undocumented jobs in the West, be paid a fraction of the going wage with no benefits, live in crowded quarters, and have no legal rights, because:

    (a)   culturally they aspire to be in the West.
    (b)   Western Europe is the gateway to America.
    (c)   **alternative conditions for them in their own country are even worse. (Pg 161)**
    (d)   Western Europeans welcome them with open arms.

B. Truth or False Questions

F (Pg 138)   1. Business ethics is sufficiently addressed is the MNC meets all local legal requirements.

F (Pg 139)   2. Managerial decisions are purely economic and ethical concerns are secondary.

T (Pg 144)   3. Bribery is not limited to money but may entail expensive gifts as well.

F (Pg 146)   4. The best way to avoid violations of the FCPA is to ask for receipts for everything.

T (Pg 147)   5. The FCPA is designed to prevent exorbitant bribes to high-ranking officials only.

T (Pg 149)   6. Being socially responsible goes beyond making goods at a profit, and extends to helping solve social problems as well.

F (Pg 152)   7. MNCs that do not repatriate all or most of its profits are always seen in a more favorable light by the local community.

T (Pg 153)　　8.　MNCs can become convenient targets when governments are unable to satisfy the needs and aspirations of their people.

F (Pg 159)　　9.　Most MNCs do a good job training their people for overseas assignments.

F (Pg 160)　　10.　The plight of the guest workers and illegal workers in Europe and elsewhere is largely absent in the US.

C. Short Essay Questions

1.　Distinguish between ethical and legal.

(refer to Pg 138 for initial ideas.　Also see Bhopal example Pg 150)

2.　Is being socially responsible the same as, or different from, not being socially irresponsible?　Why?

(note discussion of social responsibility on Pgs 149-150).　This could be a fun general discussion with a wide variety of perspectives.

3.　Why are managerial decisions intertwined with ethical concerns?

(refer to Pgs 139-141 for a discussion)

Chapter 6

Global Strategy Overview

Chapter Summary:

Strategy involves the critical decisions a firm makes concerning how it matches its resources and strengths with its environment in order to create an advantage over its competitors. The task of assessing a firm's strengths and weaknesses and matching them to the environment makes strategic decision-making a complicated process. In the international setting, this gets compounded as a result of the diverse environmental variables. For example, what is seen as a major strength "at home" can become a hindrance in other parts of the world.

A firm's global strategy is the result of both its efforts to create a competitive advantage for itself over other firms, and to avoid being placed at a competitive disadvantage by others. This chapter is an overview of the various strategies that a firm may choose to compete internationally. The task of achieving a competitive advantage is examined in some detail; specifically the use of a worldwide integration strategy is discussed at length. In addition, strategic decisions aimed at avoiding competitive disadvantage are also scrutinized. Porter's framework of "generic strategies" is used to help develop what the authors called "an international competitive strategies framework" as shown in Exhibit 6.3. The chapter also offers suggestions on how international firms will increasingly be organized; in particular the idea of "heterarchy" is introduced--a network of operating units where the notion of a "headquarters" carries little meaning.

Suggested Class Agenda:

To prepare for this sessions, students can be given copies of newspaper or magazine articles which depict an international firm's strategy (or they can be asked to find one in the library). For example, in the December 13, 1993 issue of *Fortune* magazine, a short article appeared discussing Citicorp's consumer banking strategy internationally. The students can be asked to consider the firm's strategy with respect to the kind of competitive advantage that it enjoys, and how it came to be. For more involved discussions, the article can be used as the base from which a discussion of the chapter's analytical model (see exhibit 6.3) may ensue. A useful variant of this approach has been to break the class into smaller groups and assign a different article to each. The class can then breakout for a short period while each group analyzes the assigned article. Afterwards, the class regroups and each group presents its findings to the rest of the class.

Depending on class composition, it may be necessary or beneficial to offer a short lecture on Porter's generic strategies, as well as his four strategies for global competition. This should be a good jumping-off point leading to a discussion of the chapter's analytical framework.

Overheads:

#1   What is Strategy?

STRATEGY:

Critical Decisions
SWOT
Create Advantage
Avoid Disadvantage
Far-Reaching Effects

#2   Integration Strategy (A)

When Appropriate?

Large Economies of Scale
Product Standardization
Low Tariff and Barriers
High Factor Cost Differences

#3   Integration Strategy (B)

When Less Attractive?

Varied Consumer Preference
Limited Economies of Scale

#4   Strategic Objectives (exhibit 6.2, Pg 197)

#5   Generic Strategies

Cost Leadership
Differentiation
Focus

#6   Global Strategies

Broad Line Global
Global Focus
National Focus
Protected Niche

#7   Competitive Strategies Framework (exhibit 6.3, Pg 205)

#8   Organization Structure to Come

Decentralized Functions Across Subs
Increasingly Strategic Role for Subs
Multiple Structures used
Integrated Operations

Discussion Questions:

1.   Identify a successful local firm and identify why it seems to have been successful (that is, its strengths). Discuss whether these strengths can be employed internationally.

Answers vary depending on the firm. However, refer to Pgs 189-199 for some ideas, especially on second part of the question.

2.   Suppose a foreign firm were seeking a joint-venture partner in your local community, discuss how the foreign firm should identify and contact potential partners.

Answers will vary, but at a minimum the students should consider the strategic objective behind this move. Moreover, the question really cannot be addressed in full until a clearer picture is developed as to the analysis that led to the foreign firm's strategic decision to go international. In addition, some attention should be paid to the discussion on quality management shown on Pg 198. Students should also anticipate reactions by local firms given this "invasion," and it is beneficial to consult Pgs 199-200 for starters. This is a far-reaching question which can take on a multitude of perspectives.

3.   Identify a firm that has been successful in international franchising and discuss the factors that account for its international success.

Answer varies depending on the firm. A good place to start would be to use exhibit 6.3 as a guide.

Test Questions:

A. Multiple Choice Questions

1.   In the past, many US firms have been able to achieve high levels of success without adopting a global perspective, because:
      (a)   of the large, affluent domestic market.
      (b)   other countries were busy rebuilding from World War II.
      (c)   lack of competitive threats from outside the US.
      (d)   all of the above.   (Pg 188)

2.   A firm's global strategy is the result of its efforts to:

      (a)   achieving a competitive advantage over its rivals.
      (b)   avoiding a competitive disadvantage.
      (c)   both (a) and (b).   (Pg 199)
      (d)   none of the above.

3.   For the international firm, global economies of scale can be a source of competitive advantage because of:

      (a)   greater differentiation of products.
      (b)   an avoidance of exchange rate fluctuations.
      (c)   higher levels of home-government assistance.
      (d)   lower production costs. (Pg 190)

4.   Often, international firms face a tradeoff between seeking competitive advantage through global economies of scale and:

      (a)   tailoring its products to specific national markets. (Pg 190)
      (b)   global downsizing.
      (c)   buying out its competition.
      (d)   all of the above.

5.   Economies of Scale may be available in:

      (a)   purchasing.
      (b)   production costs.
      (c)   marketing and logistic.
      (d)   all of the above. (Pg 190)

6.   A worldwide integration strategy may be appropriate when:

     (a)   consumer preferences are relatively homogeneous globally.
     (b)   large economies of scale are possible.
     (c)   **both (a) and (b). (Pg 192)**
     (d)   none of the above.

7.   High factor cost differences across countries and low tariffs are indications that:

     (a)   **a worldwide integration strategy may work. (Pg 192)**
     (b)   dumping is exercised by a foreign competitor.
     (c)   there is an imbalance in international trade.
     (d)   salaries need to be adjusted to reflect customer needs.

8.   The quality of the international firm's management may be the deciding factor in gaining and maintaining an advantage over competitors. Among the key dimensions of quality management are:

     (a)   a tendency to centralize all decisions.
     (b)   **an ability to shift strategies and refocus quickly when needed. (Pg 198)**
     (c)   graduate degrees in business administration.
     (d)   none of the above.

9.   Oligopolistic Reaction refers to:

     (a)   collusion by firms in an industry to set prices.
     (b)   **major firms quickly following one firm into a foreign market. (Pg 199)**
     (c)   an oligopolist's unfair trade practice against an foreign competitor.
     (d)   reactionary actions by foreign governments to nationalize industries.

10.   Porter's "generic" strategies include:

     (a)   differentiation.
     (b)   cost leadership.
     (c)   **both (a) and (b). (Pg 201)**
     (d)   none of the above.

11.   By "focus," Porter refers to:

(a)   **selecting the scope of the firm's operation, such as targeting a particular niche. (Pg 202)**

(b)   selecting a particular competitor to imitate.

(c)   emphasizing a single competitor in all your strategic decisions.

(d)   doing a good SWOT analysis.

12.   Global Focus differs from National Focus in that:

(a)   the former is an international strategy and the latter is a domestic strategy.

(b)   global focus requires at least $20 billion in sales.

(c)   national focus means competing worldwide but only in a part of the industry.

(d)   **national focus is similar to a nationally responsive strategy. (Pg 203)**

13.   The international business environment is particularly competitive because:

(a)   the domestic US market is shrinking.

(b)   **competition can come from virtually anywhere and may appear in unexpected forms. (Pg 207)**

(c)   foreign governments are to be blamed.

(d)   all of the above.

14.   A "heterarchy" refers to:

(a)   a heretofore unknown phenomenon in the global business scene.

(b)   Heter's principle with respect to how foreign markets should be entered.

(c)   **a network of operating units where the notion of a "headquarters" carries little meaning. (Pg 210)**

(d)   a hierarchy of subsidiary managers each reporting to a network of boards of directors.

15.   Increasingly, global firms will need to:

(a)   adopt a more flexible structure and give subsidiaries a more strategic role.

(b)   organize their operations in a greater variety of ways.

(c)   reduce their reliance on premeditated approach to strategic thinking.

(d)   **all of the above.   (Pg 210)**

B. True or False Questions

F (Pg 189)   1. Purely domestic firms need not concern themselves with a global perspective.

F (Pg 192)   2. By definition, international firms will always outcompete their purely domestic adversaries.

T (Pg 197)   3. A national responsiveness strategy is more conducive to local flexibility than global flexibility.

T (Pg 197)   4. Internal efficiency is a viable objective for both the worldwide integration and national responsiveness strategies.

T (Pg 198)   5. The quality of an international firm's management is a critical factor in gaining and maintaining an advantage over competitors.

F (Pg 200)   6. Having a presence in a competitor's home market is inviting an invasion by your competitors.

F (Pg 200)   7. The "triad" in global business refers to the three major industries of auto manufacturing, computer and electronics, and petroleum.

T (Pg 202)   8. Broad line global competition refers to a firm competing on a worldwide basis and offering a wide range of products in a given industry.

F (Pg 204)   9. Firms following a "protected niche" strategy seek to reinforce their defences of their business by buying out their competitors.

T (Pg 208)   10. Selecting and implementing an appropriate global strategy requires not only an understanding of the MNC's industry but also an understanding of how the MNC itself is structured and operates.

C. Short Essay Questions

1.   How can a national responsiveness strategy be used to create a competitive advantage globally?

      refer to Pgs 193-196

2.   Discuss the relationship between the generic competitive strategies and the concept of international scope.

      refer to exhibit 6.3 for a visual summary. This is a good way to facilitate a class discussion of the chapter's analytical framework.

3.   Why would global firms be likely to reduce their reliance on premeditated approaches to strategy?

      refer to Pg 210 for general ideas.

Chapter 7

The Foreign Entry Decision

Chapter Summary:

This chapter discusses the reasons why individual firms might choose to engage in international activities. These reason are categorized as reactive and proactive; however, firms may well be international for a variety of reasons, including both reactions and proactions. The chapter also provides a model of the decision making process - like any model, this is of course simplistic, but it is useful in examining the international decisions of companies. A variety of entry modes, or international options, are presented and discussed, and a firm's choice among these is related to three dimensions - company capability, location attractiveness and perceived risk. A major focus of this chapter is on the benefits and drawbacks associated with different strategic options.

The discussion on entry choice (beginning on page 242) can be used for an in-depth debate on the international entry decision. The chapter suggests some options for the eight categories, but others are possible and can be discussed in some detail. In each classification, the dimensions (CC, LA, PR) can be identified in more detail to illustrate that these cells represent simply a summary of a much more extensive analysis of the company and its environment. For example, if a country were identified as high on location attractiveness (LA), this could well be a function of availability of raw materials, costs of raw materials, low labour rates, availability of skilled labour, a well developed infrastructure, a large internal market, easy access to other desirable markets, high disposable income levels, and so on - depending on the specific details of each dimension, different entry decisions may be appropriate.

Suggested Class Agenda:

This lecture deals with the foreign entry decision. It should begin with the question: **Why do firms go overseas?** This then leads into the reactive and proactive reasons for a firm to enter the global arena.

Once the question of "Why" has been dealt with, the lecture should then proceed into a discussion of: **How do firms decide to go overseas?** The foreign entry decision making process has been summarized on Pages 227-230. The lecture should cover the six (6) questions managers should consider when contemplating a globalization move.

The next section of the lecture should answer the question: **How do firms go overseas?** This then leads the class into a discussion of foreign entry choices. The level of ownership should be discussed.

Overheads:

#1 Reacting to the Environment

        Exhibit #7.1   Page 222

#2 Seeking Competitive Advantage

        Exhibit #7.2   Page 224

#3 Foreign Entry Decision Making Process

        Question 1   *Must we be more international?*

        Question 2   *Should we become more international?*

        Question 3   *Are we capable of becoming more international?*

        Question 4   *How can we improve our capability?*

        Question 5   *What specific opportunities do we pursue?*

        Question 6   *How should we enter a specific location?*

#4 Foreign Entry Choices

       * *Exporting*

       * *Licensing*

       * *Franchising*

       * *Contracts*

       * *Turnkey Operations*

Discussion Questions:

1.   Suppose a foreign firm wants to sell its products in your local community (that is, the product will be exported from the foreign location and imported into your country), identify and discuss the regulations with which the foreign firm must comply.

     (Pages 231 to 232 from a Canadian or U.S. perspective)

2.   Identify and discuss different ways for establishing license fees.

     (Pages 232 to 234)

3.   Discuss how cultural differences are likely to affect the formation of a joint venture.

     (Look at the `what', `how much', `with whom' and `how long' of the shared aspect of joint ventures from a cultural differences point of view. Pages 237 to 239)

Test Questions:

A: Multiple Choice Questions

1. Which of the following is a proactive reason for international business:

   (a) regulations
   (b) additional resources   (Pg 223)
   (c) international competition
   (d) trade barriers

2. Some reactive reasons a company may decide to go international are:

   (a) trade barriers
   (b) customers becoming international
   (c) international competition
   (d) all of the above   (Pg 222)
   (e) a & c only

3. Which of the following is <u>not</u> a proactive reason for international business:

   (a) additional resources
   (b) synergy
   (c) power and prestige
   (d) trade barriers   (Pg 224)

4. The reasons why a company goes international include the following, <u>except</u>:

   (a) limited production ability   (Pg 220-227)
   (b) lower costs
   (c) foreign government incentives
   (d) new, expanded markets

5. All of the following can be considered as a reactive reason for a company to go international, _except_:

    (a) trade barriers
    (b) meeting international competition
    (c) seeking lower costs   (Pg 222)
    (d) existence of regulations and restrictions

6. Which of the following encompasses the most common forms of entry into a foreign country:

    (a) no foreign ownership, joint ventures, sole ownership   (Pg 230)
    (b) no foreign ownership, joint ventures, partnership
    (c) no foreign ownership, joint ventures, minority interest
    (d) no foreign ownership, joint ventures, limited partnership

7. Which choice of entry mode is relatively easy to undertake and is often the first international step for a company:

    (a) licenses
    (b) joint ventures
    (c) exports   (Pg 231)
    (d) contracts

8. All of the following statements are true about the exports, _except_:

    (a) there is no ownership involved
    (b) it is appropriate for standardized products
    (c) there are substantial operational risks involved since the company may not know anything about the host country   (Pg 232)
    (d) the exporting company can go either directly to the customer or through a home country agent
    (e) none of the above is correct about exports

9. Which of the following is considered a home country export agent:

   (a) distributors
   (b) sales branches
   (c) sales subsidiaries
   (d) export association   (Pg 232)
   (e) trade facilitation offices

10. A licensing agreement involves:

    (a) foreign direct investment
    (b) agreement to allow a foreign company to produce your products   (Pg 233)
    (c) exports and/or imports
    (d) provision of management to the foreign location
    (e) all of the above

11. Which of the following is true about licensing:

    (a) it often involves granting rights in intangible products
    (b) a licensor has to have sufficient financial and managerial capacity to undertake the license
    (c) a licensor will get royalties for compensation   (Pg 233)
    (d) if the operation is nor successful in the host country, the licensor does not suffer since it receives a fixed royalty

12. Many franchises have:

    (a) been able to retain a standardized product approach around the world
    (b) maintained international control through 100% ownership
    (c) adapted their product to local tastes   (Pg 235)
    (d) found they could ignore political risk
    (e) none of the above

13. A company considering international franchising should first:

    (a) gain experience franchising domestically   (Pg 235)
    (b) investigate competitive franchising successes
    (c) investigate the foreign market for product sales
    (d) consider the availability of joint venture partners

14. An international company seeking a joint venture partner might prefer an active partner to a silent partner because:

  (a) of additional capital needs
  (b) of the degree of control maintained
  (c) of local knowledge and influence   (Pg 237-239)
  (d) of the ready availability of partners with appropriate know-how
  (e) a company would never prefer an active joint-venture partner

15. For a large construction project in a foreign location, the most appropriate entry mode for the company is probably:

  (a) a wholly-owned subsidiary
  (b) exports
  (c) a licensing agreement
  (d) a turnkey operation   (Pg 237)

16. Which elements can be shared in a joint venture:

  (a) ownership
  (b) technology
  (c) managerial resources
  (d) potential risk
  (e) all of the above   (Pg 237-238)

17. A business where a firm provides construction of a facility, start-up and training of personnel is referred to as a :

  (a) contract
  (b) franchise
  (c) joint venture
  (d) turnkey   (Pg 237)
  (e) license

18. The factors that should be considered when making an international entry choice include:

    (a) company capability
    (b) location attractiveness
    (c) perceived risk
    (d) parent company availability
    (e) a & b
    (f) a, b & c   **(Pg 240)**
    (g) all of the above

19. What would be most appropriate in the following situation:
    high company capability, high location attractiveness and risk associated with the possibility of devaluation

    (a) a joint venture with a local company
    (b) a wholly-owned subsidiary financed by the parent
    (c) a wholly-owned subsidiary financed locally   **(Pg 266)**
    (d) do not pursue this opportunity

B: True or False Questions

F   **(Pg 219)**   1. The 600 largest transnational companies, according to UNCTNC, generated less than one-fifth of the total industrial and agricultural value as did in both the developed market economies and the developing countries.

T   **(Pg 220)**   2. The primary lines of business for the world's largest industrial and agricultural companies, petroleum & gas and machinery & equipment, accounted for approximately 49% of the total.

T   **(Pg 220)**   3. Going international for a company usually means that the firm can gain potential benefits, and also that the firm has to undertake more risk.

T   **(Pg 221)**   4. Accounting firms who set up subsidiaries to cater to established customers illustrate that some companies become international because of events outside of their immediate control.

F   **(Pg 228)**   5. Before a company decides whether it should go into international operations, it is important to assess its strengths and weaknesses because the firm's domestic strengths will provide benefits internationally.

F   **(Pg 231)**   6. In order for a company to benefit from international operations, it has to undertake a certain degree of foreign ownership.

F   **(Pg 233)**   7. Licensing agreements are important to multinationals because they must have a license to do business in a foreign country.

T   **(Pg 236)**   8. Contract agreements can be an attractive form of international entry for some companies, however, its main drawback is the short-term nature of many contracts.

T   **(Pg 239)**   9. Joint venture partners can be individuals, local companies, MNC's governments or international organizations.

F   **(Pg 238)**   10. Management does not like to enter into joint ventures in which they own less than 51% of the stock because they have no control with minority ownership.

T   **(Pg 238)**   11. Finding a good joint venture partner has been compared to finding a good marriage partner.

T   **(Pg 241)**   12. The attractiveness of a particular location will depend on the specific company. What is attractive to one company may be meaningless to another.

T   **(Pg 242)**   13. In determining the degree of involvement that it wishes in a particular location, a company might consider the size of the country's population and type of government currently in power.

C: Short Essay Questions

1. Discuss the reactive reasons firms go overseas.

    (Pgs 221-223)

2. Disucss how firms attempt to gain competitive advantage by going overseas.

    (Pgs 223-227)

3. How do firms make the decision to go overseas.

    (Pgs 227-230)

Chapter 8

Implementing Foreign Entry Decisions

Chapter Summary:

This chapter looks at the practicalities associated with various strategic choices. The entry options identified in the previous chapter are each examined in terms of the activities needed to implement these choices. There is only a limited amount of detail possible given space constraints, but this chapter should illustrate the fact that any choice involves many details if it is to be put into effect. Students can be asked to collect real documents associated with exports, licenses, ownership agreements, and so on (or the professor can develop a selection of these documents) to provide realistic information for the class.

Suggested Class Agenda:

This class is an extension of the class on Chapter 7. The professor may want to combine the two classes if time permits. This class should begin with a brief review of the material covered in Chapter 7. Then move into a discussion of the four options available for exporters. The discussion of each of these options should include the advantages and disadvantages of each option.

The next part of the lecture should centre on the other issues exporters must face. The issues to discuss are transportation, methods of payments, documentation, and product preparation. It may be helpful to use actual bills of lading, commercial invoices, different currencies, and actual products which have been prepared for export. The use of these "props" may enhance the discussion with the students.

The lecture should then continue into a discussion of licenses, contracts, and franchises. This material was covered briefly in Chapter 7, but this discussion should be in more depth. The professor may want to cover this material in more depth in the lecture on Chapter 7 so as not to break the continuity.

The level of ownership opted for by the business should be the next section of the lecture. It may be helpful to split the class up into five (5) groups and assign them one of the ownership options: total ownership, public sale of shares, ownership fadeout, little ownership, and joint ventures. The groups should describe the ownership option and provide advantages and disadvantages of each. They then report back to the class with their findings.

The final portion of the lecture should be centered on strategic alliances. The role of a strategic alliance as a foreign entry option will likely bring up the issue of cooperation. This can then lead into a discussion of ethics.

Overheads:

#1 Export Intermediary Options

     (i)   Direct from Exporter to Foreign Buyer
     (ii)   From Exporter, through a Domestic Export Intermediary, to Foreign Buyer
     (iii) From Exporter, through a Foreign Import Intermediary, to Foreign Buyer
     (iv)   From Exporter, through Domestic Export Intermediary, to Buyer

#2   Direct from Exporter to Foreign Buyer

    Benefits

        costs minimized
        direct communication
        internal export skills
        familiarity with export markets
        dominance of exporter's interest

    Drawbacks

        require internal specialists
        cost of internal specialists
        financial risk

#3 From Exporter, through a Domestic Export Intermediary, to Foreign Buyer

> ### *Benefits*
>
> > *outside expertise utilized*
> > *good working relationships*
> > *free up internal resources*
> > *transfer of financial risk*

> ### *Drawbacks*
>
> > *conflict of interests*
> > *no development of internal expertise*
> > *cost of intermediary*
> > *lack of in-depth knowledge*

#4 From Exporter, through a Foreign Import Intermediary, to Foreign Buyer

> ### *Benefits*
>
> > *specialized knowledge provided*
> > *intermediary has contacts*

> ### *Drawbacks*
>
> > *communication barriers*
> > *provide export expertise*
> > *cost of intermediary*

#5 From Exporter, through Domestic Export Intermediary, to Buyer

#6 Transportation Issues

> > * *Air*
> > * *Land*
> > * *Sea*

#7 Payment Methods

> * *Currency*
>
> * *Credit*

#8 Documentation

> * *Bills of Lading*
> * *Commercial Invoices*
> * *Export Licences*
> * *Insurance Certificates*
> * *Certificates of Product Origin*
> * *Inspection Certificates*
> * *Payment Documents*

#9 Ownership Options

> (i)   *Total Ownership*
> (ii) *Public Sale of Shares*
> (iii) *Ownership Fadeout*
> (iv) *Joint Ventures*

Discussion Questions:

1. Suppose a foreign firm wants to sell its products in your local community (that is, the product will be exported from the foreign location and imported into your country), identify and discuss the regulations with which the foreign firm must comply.

    (This will require substantial outside work. Students need to contact customs official, customs brokers and so on. Specifics should be identified in terms of packaging, standards, labelling, and so on).

2.   Identify and discuss different ways for establishing license fees.

      (This will require library research to identify different possibilities. Students should explore a variety of options - e.g. fees based on sales, profits, units; fixed fees versus variable fees; fees changing over time. The aim is to have students recognize that different license fees are appropriate for different situations).

3.   Discuss how cultural differences are likely to affect the formation of a joint-venture.

      (Students should be able to answer this based on information in the text. Students should examine cultural variations - e.g. Hofstede's model - and relate these variations to aspects of joint venture formation - e.g. negotiations, objectives, trust, communication, motivation, and so on).

Test Questions:

A: Multiple Choice Questions

1. Which of the following is <u>not</u> an alternative export route:

   (a) direct from exporter to foreign buyer
   (b) from exporter, through a foreign import, to foreign buyer
   (c) from exporter, through a domestic export intermediary to foreign buyer
   (d) from exporter through foreign exporter to foreign buyer   <u>(Pg 251)</u>

2. Exports/Imports are practically more complex then many people realize. An exporter should consider:

   (a) export documentation
   (b) foreign import regulations
   (c) when the establishment of a subsidiary is advantageous
   (d) a & b
   (e) all of the above   <u>(Pg 251)</u>

3. From an exporter's point of view, what is the advantage of the following export route: *exporter, foreign import intermediary, foreign buyer*

   (a) development of internal expertise
   (b) the exporter must provide export expertise   <u>(Pg 253)</u>
   (c) the exporter does not know much about the foreign buying firm, which may not be a competent importer
   (d) the foreign intermediary has broad contact with a variety of parties

4. Which of the following is generally true about sea transportation:

   (a) it is usually a direct route
   (b) it is safer and more reliable then air transportation
   (c) it is appropriate for products of varying sizes and weights   <u>(Pg 254)</u>
   (d) it is a versatile means of transportation
   (e) all of the above

5. When exporting goods, transportation choices involve trade-offs in terms of:

    (a) cost, speed and safety
    (b) reliability, convenience and costs
    (c) speed, safety, reliability and costs
    (d) all of the above   (Pg 254)

6. Which of the following are major concerns regarding product preparation for a foreign country:

    (i)   foreign regulation requirements
    (ii) language
    (iii) packaging for transportation
    (iv) distribution methods

    (a) i, ii & iii   (Pg 257-258)
    (b) i, ii & iv
    (c) ii, iii & iv
    (d) i, ii, iii & iv

7. A firm, as owner or licensor of the particular technology, needs to consider the following issue prior to entering into a licensing agreement:

    (a) whether the licensee is trustworthy and capable of using the licensed asset effectively
    (b) payment terms and time frame
    (c) protection of licensed assets through legal means
    (d) all of the above   (Pg 258-259)
    (e) a & b

8. Licensing a foreign company would necessarily involve:

    (a) legal protection of patents, copyrights and trademarks
    (b) granting rights to patents, copyrights or trademarks   (Pg 259)
    (c) providing services based on expertise
    (d) obtaining ownership through stock purchase

9. Which of the following firms needs to be particularly culturally sensitive because the nature of their business necessitates most cross-cultural interactions:

    (a) exporters of heavy machinery
    (b) contractors for managerial services   (Pg 260)
    (c) licensor of the firm's trademark
    (d) turnkey operation for a construction project

10. Many firms have chosen to franchise internationally because:

    (a) they have a well established image   (Pg 261)
    (b) they have tested the international market through exports
    (c) they have concluded that a public sale of shares internationally is not feasible
    (d) international managers generally prefer franchising

11. What is the major <u>disadvantage</u> of total ownership?

    (a) increased political risk
    (b) control may be maintained by the parent
    (c) the firm may not get a fair share of profit
    (d) all of the above
    (e) a & b   (Pg 263)

12. Which entry method into a foreign market provides the most decision-making control of operations in a foreign location:

    (a) contracting
    (b) ownership   (Pg)263
    (c) joint venture
    (d) none of the above

13. Ownership fade-out involves:

    (a) exiting a host country
    (b) selling of shares over time   (Pg 265)
    (c) hiring nationals
    (d) owners taking a less visible profile

14. Ideally, joint ventures provide:

    (a) reduced risk and fast decisions
    (b) reduced risk and synergy   (Pg 267)
    (c) increased skill levels and reduced capitalization
    (d) few disputes and increased responsiveness to problems

15. In recent years, joint ventures have become reasonably common in international business because:

    (a) it blends the partners' respective strengths
    (b) it can improve a company's local image
    (c) Japanese companies prefer joint ventures
    (d) all of the above
    (e) a & b   (Pg 266-268)

16. A partnership involving shared ownership is known as:

    (a) a strategic alliance
    (b) an ownership fade out
    (c) a joint venture   (Pg 266)
    (d) an international share agreement

17. Disadvantages of choosing the host government as a joint venture partner includes:

    (a) the fate of the joint venture is often associated with the ups and downs of the government
    (b) there is greater risk that the joint venture will be nationalized
    (c) the government is not structured for the same kind of decision making as the private business firm
    (d) all of the above   (Pg 268)
    (e) a & c

18. If a company wants to retain a fair amount of control over the foreign operation and also to improve its local image, what approach seems more appropriate:

    (a) wholly-owned subsidiary
    (b) joint venture with host government as the partner
    (c) joint venture with a silent local private firm as the partner   (Pg 269)
    (d) joint venture with an active local private firm as the partner
    (e) joint venture with an MNC from a third country as the partner

19. To be successful, a joint venture should probably have which of the following:

    (a) clear defined goals
    (b) established measures of performance
    (c) well-defined parent contributions
    (d) all of the above   (Pg 270-272)
    (e) a & b
    (f) none of the above

20. Which of the following is/are true of a strategic alliance:

    (a) they can be described as any cooperative venture between two or more organizations
    (b) they involve many of the same problems as traditional joint ventures
    (c) they eliminate some of the problems associated with loss of firm specific advantages
    (d) they are generally safer than joint ventures
    (e) a & b   (Pg 273)
    (f) c & d

21. Accusations of unethical behaviour by international firms:

    (a) have included violations of human rights and harm to infants
    (b) can have negative and wide ranging repercussions
    (c) are generally false
    (d) cannot be substantiated
    (e) all of the above
    (f) a & b   (Pg 275-278)
    (g) c & d

B: True or False Questions

F   <u>(Pg 250)</u>   1. Exports/Imports are usually the initial step for companies to do international business, but they become unimportant when companies become involved in other forms of entry, such as joint ventures, licensing, etc...

F   <u>(Pg 251)</u>   2. Of the four export routes, the direct route from exporter to foreign buyer is the best choice because of lower costs.

F   <u>(Pg 255)</u>   3. Payment methods are not particularly important to importers because these are usually handled by banks.

T   <u>(Pg 257)</u>   4. The appropriate packaging associated with exports will depend on the product, the method of transportation and the country to which the product is shipped.

F   <u>(Pg 258)</u>   5. From the licensor's viewpoint, the most critical considerations are payment terms and time frames, while protection of licensed assets is only a minor factor because the licensee will obtain the technology through the license anyway.

T   <u>(Pg 261)</u>   6. Franchising is more common in the United States than elsewhere in the world.

F   <u>(Pg 263)</u>   7. Japanese companies generally avoid wholly-owned subsidiaries because they do not like the degree of control associated with this ownership option.

F   <u>(Pg 265)</u>   8. The greatest advantage to an ownership fadeout agreement is that the company eliminates the need for control over time.

F   <u>(Pg 268)</u>   9. Generally speaking, choosing the host government as a joint venture partner is better than choosing a host private firm because the government is expected to exert its power to smooth the way for the joint venture.

F   <u>(Pg 270)</u>   10. Joint ventures between MNCs are very uncommon because they are generally competitors.

T   <u>(Pg 271)</u>   11. When forming a joint venture, small companies are vulnerable to having their expertise lost to larger partners.

T   <u>(Pg 271)</u>   12. Companies with similar cultures and relatively equal financial resources tend to work well together in joint venture.

F   <u>(Pg 272)</u>   13. To be successful, a joint venture should always set long term goals before entering into the agreement. The longevity of the enterprise is usually the best measure for the joint venture's success.

F   <u>(Pg 273)</u>   14. A strategic alliance is less risky than a joint venture since there is no shared ownership involved.

T   <u>(Pg 274)</u>   15. No matter which form of entry a company chooses, the company's interactions with the host government are almost inevitable and these interactions are an on-going process.

C: Short Essay Questions

1. Identify the major concerns of exporters and discuss the options available to an exporter for one of these issues.

        Major concerns -
* **export routes**	<u>**(Pgs 250-254)**</u>
* **transportation**	<u>**(Pgs 254-255)**</u>
* **payment methods**	<u>**(Pg 255)**</u>
* **export documentation**	<u>**(Pgs 256-257)**</u>
* **product preparation**	<u>**(Pgs 257-258)**</u>

2. Discuss the concept of franchising and the elements that make for a successful international franchise.

<u>**(Pgs 261-262)**</u>

3. Strategic Alliances are becoming much more common in today's international companies. Identify five (5) reasons fro avoiding such alliances.

   Reasons -

   * loss of technology to partner
   * brain-drain from smaller partner to larger
   * difficulty of measuring success if partners have opposing views
   * difficulty of reaching decisions because two groups have to agree
   * potential conflicts due to different objectives
   * sharing of profits could mean lower returns
   * partner's activities, nationality, etc.., may reflect negatively on your company and strategic alliance
   * lack of trust between partners make activities difficult
   * dissolving agreements can be a problem, particularly if only one partner desires it

   <u>(Pgs 273-274)</u>

Chapter 9

Adapting Management to Foreign Environments

Chapter Summary

This chapter examined three models used in cultural analysis. The chapter discussed the Hofstede VSM, the Kluckhohn and Strodtbeck Value Orientation Model, and the Ronen and Shenkar Country Clusters. Each model was discussed in turn and its contribution to global management explored. The chapter also points out the limitations of using such models. Limitations such as the inherent Western bias and the exclusive focus on national culture are explored. It is important that global managers understand the significance of cultural values. Since cultural values pervade a firm's decision marking process, it is vital that managers are cognisant of the relationship of culture and management.

Suggested Class Agenda:

The class can begin with a brief review of the material in Chapter 3, particularly the definition of culture. Then the class should explore the meaning of cultural values.

The majority of the class will be spent discussing the three models used in cultural analysis. The first model, Hofstede's Value Survey Model should be described and the four dimensions explained. Exhibit 9.2 will provide a good start to the discussion on the limitation of the model and its relevance to global managers. The second model, Kluckhohn and Strodtbeck's Value Orientation Model, should also be described and the five common problems explained. The discussion should turn to the question: **What does this mean to global firms?** The discussion of the final model, Ronen and Shenkar's Country Clusters, may be enhanced with the assistance of Exhibits 9.4 and 9.6.

Overheads:

#1   Cultural Values

> *Values*
> *Needs*
> *Attitudes*
> *Norms*

#2   Hofstede's Value Survey Model (VSM)

> *4 Dimensions*

> > *Individualism*   *(IDV)*
> > *Uncertainty voidance*   *(UAI)*
> > *Power Distance*   *(PDI)*
> > *Masculinity*   *(MAS)*

#3   Kluckhohn and Strodtbeck's Value Orientation Model

> *Common Problem Areas*

> > *Relationship to Nature*
> > *Time Orientation*
> > *Basic Human Nature*
> > *Activity Orientation*
> > *Human Relationships*

#4   Country Clusters

> *Exhibit 9.4   Page 306*

> *Exhibit 9.6   Page 309*

Discussion Questions:

1. Select one of Hofstede's cultural value dimensions (for example, individualism). Identify two countries that are at opposite extremes on these two dimensions - one high and one low. Discuss how this difference would be likely to show up in a meeting between managers of these two countries.

    (Answers will vary depending on the cultural value dimension and countries which are chosen. All answers should begin with a discussion of the chosen dimension {Pgs 291-301}.)

2. Suppose you have been asked to design a training program for employees in a foreign subsidiary of your firm. Computers are being introduced to these employees and your initial task is to train the employees in a basic use of computers. You have done some research and you have found that people in the foreign location are usually oriented to the past and see their relationship to nature as one of subjugation. Discuss how these cultural characteristics would influence the training program.

    (This is a basic discussion of culture, culture value dimensions and value orientations from Pages 301 to 304)

3. *"A group of local Brazilian accountants working for the ABC corporation in Brazil will behave in the same way."* Discuss the validity of this statement.

    (A discussion of the heterogeneity of culture is called for from Pages 313-318)

Test Questions:

A: Multiple Choice Questions

1. In designing jobs, autonomy and variety should be increased when which of the following is the case:

   (a) IDV is high and UAI is low   (Pgs 291-4)
   (b) IDV is low and UAI is high
   (c) MAS is low and UAI is low
   (d) PDI is high and MAS is low

2. The belief that all people should have equal rights and the opportunity to change their position in society is prevalent when:

   (a) the power distance index is low   (Pg 294)
   (b) the equality distance index is high
   (c) the risk avoidance index is high
   (d) the masculinity index is high
   (e) the uncertainty avoidance index is high
   (f) none of the above

3. Risk taking is encouraged and job security not stressed when:

   (a) the individual index is high
   (b) the uncertainty avoidance index in low   (Pg 293)
   (c) the femineity index is high
   (d) the individuality index is low

4. Uncertainty avoidance is:

   (a) one measure of cultural values   (Pg 293)
   (b) a theory of international investment
   (c) part of the mercantilist theory
   (d) none of the above

5. According to Hofstede's Value Survey Module (VSM) there are four dimensions to culture. They are labelled:

    (a) collectivism, risk avoidance, masculinity, power distance
    (b) individualism, uncertainty avoidance, masculinity, power distance <u>**(Pgs 291-294)**</u>
    (c) collectivism, uncertainty avoidance, femininity, equality distance
    (d) individualism, risk avoidance, femininity, power distance

6. Which of the following is likely:

    (i) *When individualism is high, the society is less concerned about social harmony*
    (ii) *When uncertainty avoidance is high, the society is unconcerned about certainty and security*
    (iii) *If PDI is low, the prevalent belief is that all people should have equal rights*

    (a) i & iii   <u>**(Pgs 291-294)**</u>
    (b) ii & iii
    (c) i & ii
    (d) iii

7. Which of the following is not considered a traditional male value:

    (a) achievement orientation
    (b) concern for the environment   <u>**(Pg 293)**</u>
    (c) desire for material possessions
    (d) assertiveness

8. A paternalistic leader would be appropriate in countries with the following value profile:

    (a) high IDV/low UAI
    (b) high MAS/high PDI
    (c) low IDV/high PDI   <u>**(Pg 296)**</u>
    (d) low PDI/high UAI

9. Based on Hofstede's model, how would you classify the North American culture?

    (a) low power distance
    (b) high individualism
    (c) moderately high masculinity
    (d) all of the above   (Pg 295)
    (e) a & c

10. Hofstede found that Japan was:

    (a) individualistic and concerned with social good
    (b) low on uncertainty avoidance
    (c) high on masculinity   (Pg 295)
    (d) low on power distance

11. The Anglo cluster of countries is generally:

    (a) high on individualism and relatively low on power distance   (Pg 295)
    (b) high on individualism and low on uncertainty avoidance
    (c) high on individualism and low on masculinity
    (d) high on individualism and high on power distance

12. The relationship of human to nature deals with:

    (a) the past, the present and the future
    (b) one person's involvement with another
    (c) good versus evil
    (d) giving in, working with, and conquering   (Pg 301)

13. Which of the following is <u>not</u> one of Kluckhohn & Strodtbeck's Value Orientations:

    (a) relationships of humans to nature
    (b) human's cultural precepts   (Pg 301)
    (c) human's time orientation
    (d) human's activity orientation

14. According to Kluckhohn & Strodtbeck, North Americans would most likely:

   (a) view many events as inevitable
   (b) want to conquer natural phenomenon   (Pg 301)
   (c) try to preserve nature as it is
   (d) none of the above is true of North Americans
   (e) a & b

15. Anthropologists Kluckhohn & Strodtbeck view cultural similarities and differences in terms of FIVE basic problems. Identify which of the following is/are correct:

   (i)   *humans to nature relationship - subjugation, mastery and harmony*
   (ii) *human's time orientation - long term and short term*
   (iii) *basic human nature - evil, good and mixed*
   (iv) *human relationships - individual, lineal and co-lineal*

   (a) i, ii & iii
   (b) i, ii & iv
   (c) i, iii & iv   (Pgs 301-303)
   (d) all of the above statements are correct

16. In a society that believes in the basic goodness of humans, which of the following would be most likely:

   (a) reinforcement management
   (b) participative management   (Pg 303)
   (c) bureaucratic systems
   (d) collective rewards

B: True or False Questions

F   **(Pg 306)**   1.   The Latin European cluster of countries includes Germany, Austria and France

F   **(Pg 308)**   2.   According to the cultural antecedents in the country clusters presented in the text, the Latin European group is most similar to the Anglo group.

F   **(Pg 291)**   3. A society which is collective, does not avoid uncertainty, believes in power distinctions and is relatively low on masculinity suggests that an achievement-oriented, money-based reward system and a flat organizational structure would be effective.

T   **(Pg 293)**   4. A society which is individualistic, avoids uncertainty and believes in equality and traditional male values is likely to encourage individuals to make decisions and compete, while emphasizing job security.

T   **(Pg 294)**   5. New Zealand as a society is individualistic, does not avoid uncertainty, and believes in equality and traditional male values.

T   **(Pg 296)**   6. In Japan, a paternalistic leadership style would probably be appropriate, given Japan's score on Hofstede's dimensions.

F   **(Pg 296)**   7. Based on a study conducted by Punnett and Withane (1989), managers of fast food restaurants in North America are typically represented by the value profile of the prevalent Anglo culture.

C: Short Essay Questions:

1. Identify the four dimensions of Hofstede's model and discuss their relationship to organizational management.

(Pgs 291-294)

2. Identify and explain Kluckhohn and Strodbeck's value orientations.

(Pgs 301-305)

3. Select one of Hofstede's dimensions and discuss how it would likely influence planning and decision making in an organization.

(Pgs 291-301)

Chapter 10

Managing Operations Globally

Chapter Summary:

This chapter looks at operational decisions from an international perspective. It begins by distinguishing between goods and services because it is felt that decisions regarding physical facilities and the movement of inputs and outputs might well differ for the two categories. The growing importance of services in the world economy makes this distinction of particular interest, and it can be referred to throughout the discussion of this chapter. To a large extent, however, this chapter focuses on operational decisions as they apply to goods and not services.

An overview of the operational system is presented in this chapter and can be useful in introducing the topic and explaining the issues to be discussed. This discussion of decisions includes dealing with procurement or sourcing, production issues (including location, type and coordination of facilities), delivery of the final product to customers, and logistical networks which encompass the entire operational system. Throughout the chapter the question is raised regarding the international dimensions of these decisions. Specifically we ask: ***"How do operational issues change because they are international?"*** The trade-offs between unified, rationalized global operations and fragmented, nationally adapted local operations is a particularly important consideration in all these operational decisions.

Suggested Class Agenda:

This lecture should be divided into three sections. Each section should cover one the three main issues in Chapter 10: procurement, production, and delivery. The first section, procurement, is identified as having three main issues to cover. The first issue is the "buy-or-make" decision. This discussion of the degree of vertical integration is enhanced by Exhibit 10.1. It is helpful to sue this exhibit as it succinctly details the benefits and drawbacks of either decision. The second issue is national origin. The discussion here should center on the national origin of suppliers and the ramification for global firms in general and procurement departments specifically. The final issue is timing and is directed towards the sending and receiving of supplies.

The second section of the lecture looks at production issues. Specifically, it looks at three issues. The first issue is product quality which will lead to a discussion of TQM. The professor should define TQM and discuss the costs and benefits of implementing TQM system. It is also important to point out the costs associated with not implementing TQM. A second issue is the location of production facilities. The main question here is: **Do we locate close to our markets or to our inputs?** This will lead into a debate of the costs of benefits of each choice. At the same time the professor will want to discuss the advantages and drawbacks of a concentrated versus a dispersed location strategy. The final issue is the type of facility the firm will need. The decision is predicated on four characteristics: climatic, cultural, physical, and governmental. Each should be discussed in turn.

The final section of the lecture examines delivery or logistical issues. This section can be quite complex or quite simple depending on the type of logistical system the professor wishes to discuss. The main issue is that firms want a low-cost, reliable distribution system to move their inputs and outputs.

Overheads:

#1   Degree of Integration

Exhibit #10.1   Page 325

#2   Total Quality Management (TQM)

"The international firm achieves TQM by identifying both similarities and distinctions in its worldwide operations and uses these to create quality"

#3 Location of Facilities

	Benefits	*Costs*
Concentrated	*efficiency* *standardization*	*reliance on one* *location*
Dispersed	*adaptation* *flexibility*	*high per-unit cost* *increase administrative* *complexity*

#4 Types of Facilities

> *Climatic*
> *Cultural*
> *Physical*
> *Governmental*

Discussion Questions: **Note: these are the same as Chapter 8**

1. Both goods and services can be imported and exported. Identify and discuss some of the likely differences in exporting a good (physical product) versus a service.

   (Begin this answer with a discussion of the differences between a good and a service {Pgs 340-342}. Then move into a identification and discussion of export decision strategies {Pgs 250-254}.)

2. Discuss how the North American Free Trade Agreement is likely to influence decisions regarding facility locations within the North American region.

   (Begin with a discussion of the entry decision and how NAFTA will change their entry decision {Pgs 240-241}. Next speak about the effect on location {Pgs 333-335}.)

3. Assume you are exporting a perishable product from the United States to the People's Republic of China. Identify the various options available and discuss the advantages and disadvantages of each.

   (Discuss export strategies and specifically address the issue of timeliness {Pgs 250-254}.)

Test Questions:

A: Multiple Choice Questions

1. Which of the following is true of operational management:

   (a) sometimes it takes a long-term view, and at other times a short-term view (Pg 323)
   (b) it is generally long-term rather than short-term
   (c) it is generally short-term rather than long-term
   (d) it is more efficient if long-term priorities take precedence over short-term ones
   (e) b & d

2. Which of the following is true of goods and services:

   (a) the difference between the two categories is generally easy to identify
   (b) the two categories can be closely connected
   (c) services are often of a personal nature
   (d) because of their personal nature, expectations regarding service levels do not differ very much around the world
   (e) all of the above
   (f) a & c   (Pg 340)
   (g) c & d

3. Service characteristics are:

   (a) the attributes associated with a particular service   (Pg 341)
   (b) generally easier to standardize than service levels
   (c) more important internationally than service levels
   (d) the quality level demand of a particular service
   (e) all of the above
   (f) a & c
   (g) c & d

4. According to trade statistics on goods and services, which of the following is true:

   (a) goods are becoming relatively more important than services
   (b) services are an increasingly important component of the world's economy
   (c) trade in services has increased dramatically in recent years
   (d) an increase in trade in goods is usually accompanied by a decrease in trade in services
   (e) a & d
   (f) b & c   (Pg 324)
   (g) none of the above

5. The degree to which a firm is its own supplier and market is described in terms of:

   (a) horizontal integration
   (b) vertical integration   (Pg 325)
   (c) production rationalization
   (d) procurement decisions

6. If a company is said to have a high degree of vertical integration in terms of procurement, it means that:

   (a) the firm makes almost all of its own inputs   (Pg 325)
   (b) the firm buys almost all of its own inputs
   (c) the firm sells its products to other distributors
   (d) the firm markets its products directly at consumers

7. Which of the following are advantages of making a firm's own inputs:

   (a) avoid business risks
   (b) avoid learning about suppliers
   (c) decreased need for expertise and investment
   (d) control over delivery   (Pg 325)

8. Which of the following are disadvantages of buying a firm's own inputs:

   (a) more reliance on outsiders   (Pg 325)
   (b) less need to compete for supplies
   (c) greater need for investment
   (d) overspecialization

9. The fact that the United States is one of the few countries in the world that does not use the metric system of measurement can:

    (a) lead to consumer boycotts against U.S. products
    (b) be crucial when dealing with precision parts **(Pg 328)**
    (c) often result in frustrating interactions involving third countries in operational decisions
    (d) means that two sets of books need to be maintained by U.S. firms

10. A system which keeps no inventory on hand is referred to as a(n):

    (a) efficiency inventory system
    (b) inventory timed system
    (c) just-in-time inventory system **(Pg 330)**
    (d) just-in-time production system
    (e) none of the above

11. The choice of location for a firm's facilities would likely take which of the following into consideration:

    (a) sources of supply and markets
    (b) the ease with which inputs and final products can be moved
    (c) the size and weight of finished products
    (d) the need to preserve freshness
    (e) all of the above **(Pg 334)**
    (f) a, b & c

12. A dispersed production strategy would be most likely for a(n):

    (a) international firm with a focus on efficiency
    (b) international firm specializing in services
    (c) international firm with a multi-domestic strategy and structure **(Pg 335)**
    (d) global firm with a global strategy

13. In choosing a plant site, management should:

    (a) select one where skilled labour is available
    (b) select one where production and transportation costs are minimized (Pg 334)
    (c) choose one where land and labour costs are lowest
    (d) choose a site near to major markets

14. All of the following statements are advantages of a dispersed production strategy, <u>except</u>:

    (a) flexibility
    (b) adaptation
    (c) less coordination effort   (Pg 337)
    (d) taking advantage of the least-cost inputs

B: True or False Questions

F   (Pg 323)   1. Operational decisions focus on short-term decisions rather then long-term decisions.

T   (Pg 341)   2. Due to the different characteristics of good & services, services often need more adaptation and modification for foreign markets.

F   (Pg 340)   3. The term product, as used in the text, refers to goods rather than services.

T   (Pg 325)   4. Vertical decisions are make-versus-buy trade-offs.

F   (Pg 325)   5. One disadvantage of buying inputs is the increased choice among suppliers.

T   (Pg 327)   6. Decisions about sourcing can have negative impact because of politics in the sourcing country.

F   (Pg 327)   7. Suppliers from different locations usually avoid variations in quality and service, therefore cost is the prime consideration.

T   (Pg 330)   8. Production systems with just-in-time delivery are vulnerable to transportation delays.

F   (Pg 331)   9. International companies should develop efficient operational networks based on scientific linear programming models, rather than on subjective judgements.

T   (Pg 334)   10. Many products are often assembled in poorer countries because of the relatively low mobility of labour.

F   (Pg 335)   11. A dispersed strategy of production facilities is appropriate for the production of standardized products.

F   (Pg 337)   12. Production strategy and design of production facilities are two clearly separate issues in operations management.

F   (Pg 338)   13. It is not likely that designers would need to take cultural factors into account in the design of production facilities.

T   (Pg 339)   14. Logistical systems are only as good as their weakest link.

F   (Pg 339)   15. In today's global environment, effective and reliable transportation systems are generally available no matter where a firm operates.

C: Short Essay Questions

1. Differentiate between goods and services, using examples to illustrate the differences.

(Pgs 340-342)

2. Describe an imaginary parent-subsidiary relationship and discuss how the objectives of the parent and subsidiary might differ.

(Pgs 326-327)

3. Identify and explain the importance of national origin in a firm's selection of suppliers.

(Pgs 328-329)

4. Discuss the likely relationship between a global or multi-domestic strategy and production strategies.

(Pgs 335-337)

Chapter 11

Organizing and Control in Global Organizations

Chapter Summary:

This chapter considers questions associated with maintaining control of an international firm. A variety of issues associated with control are considered, beginning with a discussion of the characteristics associated with effective control systems, and examining how these apply in an international firm. This is followed by consideration of various types of controls such as accounting and auditing, plans, policies and procedures. Each of these types of control are then examined in terms of how they change when a firm becomes international. The chapter also looks at some special issues of control, information systems, performance evaluation, and organizational structure. Throughout this chapter we are looking at control issues which are equally important in domestic firms. We basically ask: ***"How does this change when a firm is international?"*** This question can be posed to students and the content of the chapter discussed in this way.

The sections of the chapter dealing with structure try to illustrate the variety of structures that can exist. It is important to stress that these are essentially `models'. Each organization will likely be a variation of one of these. Looking at the actual structure of international organizations can help illustrate this point.

Suggested Class Agenda:

This lecture covers two main topics: organizational structure and organizational control. It is important to stress that the structuring of organizations is related to the organizational control process.

The first topic, organizational structure, is best begun by examining the development of typical North American International companies. The lecture should cover the four stages in this development and the ramifications of each stage. This first topic should be concluded through a discussion of the relationship of structure to control

The second topic is more involved than the first topic. The issue of control should be introduced through a discussion of the characteristics of what could be termed an effective control system. Then the steps involved in a control system should be examined. The final portion of the lecture should cover the many ways a company can control operations. First a review of how accounting and auditing procedures can affect control is in order. Second, the lecture should describe the use of plans, procedures, and policies. The professor should also cover the advantages and disadvantages of these mechanisms. Finally, a debate of bureaucratic versus corporate culture and centralization versus decentralization should round out the class.

Overheads:

    #1   Development of North American International Companies

                Export Structures   *Exhibit 11.1*   *Page 351*

                International Division *Exhibit 11.2*   *Page 352*

                Global Structure   *Exhibit 11.3*   *Page 353*

                Multi-Dimensional Structure

    #2   Types of Global Structures

                Global Functional Structure

                Global Product Structure

                Global Area Structure

    #3 Characteristics of an Effective Control System

                i. Accuracy
                ii. Timeliness
                iii. Objectivity
                iv. Acceptability
                v. Understandability
                vi. Cost Effectiveness
                vii. Firm Specificity

#4   Control System Basic Steps

Decide Final Results
Identify Interim Results
Establish Standards
Collect Data
Compare to Standards
Identify Deviation Causes
Corrective Action
Compare Actuals to Expectations
Review Plans and Goals

#5   Control Mechanisms

Accounting
Auditing
Plans
Procedures
Policies
Bureaucracy
Corporate Culture
Centralization
Decentralization

#6   Centralization versus Decentralization

Industry Factors
Type of Subsidiary
Functional Factors
Parent Philosophy
Parent Confidence in Subsidiary
Cultural Similarity
Firm Specific Advantage

Discussion Questions:

1.   Discuss how the formation of regional trading blocks is likely to be reflected in the organizational structures of international firms.

      (Regional trading blocks are groups of countries with few barriers to trade within the group. Trade barriers within the block are low and regulations regarding advertising, etc. is standardized - company structure will reflect this through importance of export division or international division because trade within the block should increase. In addition, operations will be rationalized as far as possible to serve the entire region from one location, this will mean larger plants and adoption of standardized approaches for the region. There are likely to be greater differences between trading blocks and thus a need for different approaches for each region, this likely means a global regional structure would be appropriate.)

2.   Discuss how a strategy of global rationalization is likely to be reflected in a firm's choice of international organizational structure.

      (Pages 349 to 357)

3.   In a multi-domestic firm (i.e. one that operates each national subsidiary as a separate entity), identify and discuss some of the challenges associated with achieving effective control.

      (Pages 364 to 372)

Test Questions:

A: Multiple Choice Questions

1. Control is fundamental to effective to operations in any organization, but it is of particular importance in international firms. Which of the following would contribute to a need for more control in an MNC:

    (a) internal structure may be complex
    (b) the international environment is constantly changing
    (c) a substantial degree of delegation of authority is required for effective operations
    (d) all of the above   (Pg 358)
    (e) a & b

2. **XXXX** is described as difficult to achieve in international companies because of geographic distance and cultural and national differences.

    (a) accuracy
    (b) cost effectiveness
    (c) timeliness   (Pg 360)
    (d) objectivity
    (e) none of the above is correct

3. All of the following are considered characteristics of an effective control systems, except:

    (a) timely and accurate
    (b) accurate and acceptable
    (c) subjective and personal   (Pgs 359-364)
    (d) understandable

4. Designing a control system so that organizational members will not ignore it or sabotage it focuses on which of the following:

    (a) acceptability   (Pg 361)
    (b) relevance
    (c) human effectiveness
    (d) subjective control
    (e) none of the above

5.   The concept that information is only useful if it is understandable and can be interpreted by those who use it, is referred to as the characteristic of:

  (a) objectivity
  (b) acceptability
  (c) usability
  (d) clarity   (Pg 362)
  (e) none of the above

6. Designing a control system involves which of the following:

  (a) determining desired final results
  (b) establishing standards
  (c) comparison with standards
  (d) reviewing plan for the following cycle
  (e) all of the above   (Pg 363)
  (f) a, b & c

7. Accounting and auditing in international firms is complex because:

  (a) legal requirements for reporting financial information can vary from country to country   (Pg 365)
  (b) these functions are outside of the control systems
  (c) they are often not objective
  (d) all of the above
  (e) a & b

8. Which of the following are typically used as part of a control system:

  (a) plans
  (b) policies and procedures
  (c) accounting and auditing systems
  (d) all of the above   (Pgs 365-367)
  (e) a & b

9. A **XXXXX** is a general guideline that directs decision making.

   (a) policy   (Pg 368)
   (b) procedure
   (c) guiding principle
   (d) corporate culture
   (e) none of the above

10. Which of the following firms is most likely to have a centralized control system:

   (a) Bata Shoe Organization
   (b) Pfizer Pharmaceuticals   (Pg 370)
   (c) Pillsbury
   (d) Heinz

11. Control of subsidiaries in international companies can be maintained through:

   (a) corporate culture and bureaucratic methods   (Pg 369)
   (b) personal visits and systematic reporting
   (c) complex parent-subsidiary interactions
   (d) a, b & c
   (e) most international companies do not control their subsidiaries

12. A bureaucratic control system:

   (a) moves people around the world often
   (b) has a geocentric approach to staffing
   (c) is generally highly centralized
   (d) relies on formal, explicit policies and procedures   (Pg 369)
   (e) c & d

13. Which of the following functions is likely to be most decentralized:

   (a) finance
   (b) research and development
   (c) human resources   (Pg 371)
   (d) operations

14. Which of the following is likely to have decentralized organizational control:

    (a) an oil company
    (b) a company's research and development department
    (c) a manufacturing firm
    (d) a company with a bureaucratic control system
    (e) a multi-domestic company   (Pg 372)

15. Evaluation of international manager's performance is complicated by the fact that:

    (a) some subsidiaries may not be expected to be profitable
    (b) transfer process may be used to shift profits from one location to another
    (c) process for services provided by headquarters are determined by headquarters
    (d) all of the above   (Pg 374)
    (e) none of the above

16. A multidimensional organizational structure would be most appropriate for:

    (a) a multi-domestic international company
    (b) a joint venture with an active partner
    (c) a global company with a broad product line   (Pg 355)
    (d) a regional company with a limited product line

17. Identify the most appropriate structure for a company that recognizes foreign opportunities, but is not currently anxious to pursue these:

    (a) export structure   (Pg 350)
    (b) international division
    (c) global division
    (d) multidimensional structure

18. Identify the most appropriate structure for a company that recognizes that there are opportunities which require specialized attention, but believes that there are domestic opportunities yet to be exploited:

    (a) export structure
    (b) international division   (Pg 352)
    (c) global division
    (d) multidimensional structure

19. Identify the most appropriate structure for a company that believes that international opportunities and interest have become as important as domestic opportunities:

   (a) export structure
   (b) international division
   (c) global division   **(Pg 353)**
   (d) multidimensional structure

20. An MNC with a specialized, limited product line, operating in a large number of countries would likely choose a:

   (a) global functional structure
   (b) global product structure
   (c) matrix structure
   (d) global area structure   **(Pg 354)**
   (e) an international division structure

21. Identify the most appropriate structure for a company that wants to coordinate its various product lines in many foreign locations:

   (a) export structure
   (b) international division
   (c) global division
   (d) multidimensional structure   **(Pg 355)**

B: True or False Questions

F   **(Pg 358)**   1. A complex international organization that involves substantial delegation of authority is so decentralized that controls are not necessary.

T   **(Pg 359)**   2. Although there is a particular need for control in an international firm, it is often more difficult to achieve an effective control internationally than domestically.

F   (Pg 360)   3. According to the text, clocks in Latin American countries are as accurate as those in the United States.

F   (Pg 361)   4. Objectivity in a control system means that the system will not be ignored.

T   (Pg 364)   5. Auditing information is intended largely to serve shareholders.

F   (Pg 366)   6. Black market or unreported activities are not considered acceptable anywhere in the world.

T   (Pg 366)   7. The FCPA makes black market activities on the part of a U.S. company illegal no matter where they occur.

T   (Pg 366)   8. The fact that accounting principles and policies differ from one location to another makes it difficult for international companies to compare their financial performance; but, different business practices around the world make uniform accounting practices almost impossible.

T   (Pg 370)   9. A subsidiary of a decentralized international company can have a centralized organization.

F   (Pg 370)   10. Manufacturing subsidiaries are less likely to be centrally controlled than marketing subsidiaries.

F   (Pg 374)   11. Growth in sales, market shares and profits are the most objective basis for evaluation of an international manager and these criteria should be used for performance appraisal.

T   (Pg 374)   12. Effective information systems in international companies may have to evolve over time.

T   (Pg 349)   13. An organization's structure provides a framework for the firm's control systems.

F   (Pg 357)   14. A lack of formal organization structure means a lack of organization generally.

F   (Pg 357)   15. Studies show that the formal organizational structure widely employed in North America is the most effective form of organization.

T   (Pg 358)   16. Control systems need to change to match a company's structural evolving in relation to the firm's changing strategy.

C: Short Essay Questions

1. Discuss the differences between a control system which relies on bureaucratic controls and one which relies on corporate culture.

(Pg 369)

2. Explain how product lines and countries of operation might affect an international firm's choice of structure.

(Pgs 350-355)

3. Identify and briefly explain the characteristics of an effective control system in an international firm.

(Pgs 358-364)

4. Identify and briefly explain the main factors influencing the centralization/decentralization control decision in international firms.

(Pgs 369-371)

Chapter 12

Human Resource Selection

Chapter Summary:

When a company goes international, the human resource selection challenge becomes increasingly complex. This chapter offers a selection matrix as a tool for human resource managers to consider in aiding their decision process when selecting people for overseas assignments. The chapter begins with an overview of some common terms in the international arena of human resource management: different types of employees (i.e. parent country nationals, host country nationals, third country nationals, foreign guestworkers, and expatriates) are introduced, their advantages and disadvantages analyzed, and suggestions are offered as to when each type becomes particularly appropriate.

People go through a Culture Shock Cycle when posted to overseas assignments, and the human resource manager needs to be attuned to the acculturation problems that employees face. A detailed discussion of the Culture Shock Cycle and its various stages is provided. Exhibit 12.1 (Pg 411) gives a good visual depiction of the occurrence and duration of the Cycle and its stages. It should also be noted that not all employees go through the cycle in the same manner, though evidence suggests that people do generally go through all the stages. How well an employee will be able to deal with culture shock is the subject of international adjustment, which necessitates a kind of culture learning. As this learning increases, so does the level of adjustment.

Determinants of international adjustments are introduced. Here it is useful to refer to Exhibit 12.2 (Pg 414). The degree of adjustment is a function of an interplay among the individual's own skill-sets, a non-work dimension such as cultural novelty, the job dimension, and the organizational culture. Each of these four factors is examined in detail in the chapter.

The chapter concludes with a discussion of how existing research findings may best be applied to global companies in their pursuit of excellence in human resource selection. Exhibit 12.5 (Pg 426) provides a flow chart showing a suggested selection decision process. When reviewed in conjunction with Exhibit 12.6 (Pg 430), this gives the reader helpful hints in developing a valid selection process for expatriates.

Suggested Class Agenda:

It may be a good (if perhaps a bit unconventional) idea to begin the session in a more light-hearted manner before proceeding to the "nitty-gritty" details of the selection decision process. We suggest that the concept of Culture Shock offers a good discussion point to start the session. Students can be asked beforehand to review a familiar piece of fiction (be it a book, a story, or a movie, etc.), which describes the experiences of someone going through an "overseas assignment." Examples that come to mind include James Clavell's *Shogun* and Stephen King's *Dark Tower* series. An interesting discussion should ensue regarding the Culture Shock Cycle introduced in the chapter.

A brief lecture on the various terms covered in the beginning of the chapter (eg. Parent Country Nationals, etc.) may be in order, especially if the course is offered to undergraduate students below the junior level. Depending on whether the Culture Shock Cycle "game" is implemented, the instructor may or may not decide to lecture on the cycle. But we would suggest that some coverage be given to the problems of international adjustment.

Discussion Question (2) (Pg 431) is a good way to get the class involved in a general discussion of the selection process. Perhaps the class can be broken out into smaller groups to each come up with two or three characteristics, and then after regrouping all students can participate in building the *class's* idea of the ideal international manager. The instructor may also consider expanding the scope of this question to cover non-individual aspects, and make extensive use of the four dimensions the chapter describes. This will give the discussion a richer flavor.

Overheads:

  #1 Types of International Employees

      Parent Country Nationals
      Host Country Nationals
      Third Country Nationals
      Expatriates

  #2 International Adjustment

      The degree to which the expatriate feels comfortable living and working in the host culture.

#3   Culture Shock Cycle

Exhibit 12.1, page 411.

#4   Framework of International Adjustment

Exhibit 12.2, page 414

also, expand each box into individual overhead, thus we have overheads #4, #4.1, #4.2...#4.5.

#5   Selection Process

I don't think it's a good idea to do overheads for this. Too complicated and crowded. Loses its value. Students can be asked to refer to the text.

Discussion Questions:

1.   From a student's perspective, discuss how culture shock is likely to influence a student studying in a foreign location.

           Refer to Pgs 409-413 for general ideas. If there are foreign students in the class, they may be asked to help contribute to the discussion by sharing their own experiences. For other students, the instructor may find it useful to specify a particular country where the students will hypothetically study.

2.   Select from the characteristics identified in the chapter that are important to international managers the one which you believe is most important. Discuss why this characteristic is especially important to international success as a manager.

           Answers vary. Refer to Pgs 414-419 for general ideas. Also, note "Suggested Agenda" section for some additional ideas.

3.   Discuss the relationship between effective selection of managers and culture shock.

           Here the emphasis is on international adjustment, and it is useful to refer to Pgs 409-413 to start. The discussion on the applications of research findings, Pgs 424-429, should also be useful.

Test Questions:

A. Multiple Choice Questions

1.   Parent Country Nationals refer to employees:

      (a)   whose parents are citizens of the host country.
      (b)   who are citizens of the country that headquarters the firm. (Pg 404)
      (c)   both (a) and (b).
      (d)   none of the above.

2.   When the subsidiary operates in countries high in political risk, MNCs tend to:

      (a)   sell off the subsidiary to a local firm.
      (b)   send Host Country Nationals to manage the subsidiary.
      (c)   sell off the subsidiary to the local government.
      (d)   send Parent Country Nationals to manage the subsidiary. (Pg 405)

3.   The danger of staffing overseas subsidiaries primarily with local managers is that:

      (a)   top management of North American firms will lack international experience. (Pg 406)
      (b)   local managers are much less reliable.
      (c)   local managers do not perform as well as Americans do.
      (d)   (a) and (c).

4.   An Expatriate refers to:

      (a)   someone who is responsible for sending profits from the subsidiary back to head office.
      (b)   a Host Country National.
      (c)   someone who used to be a New England Patriots fan.
      (d)   anyone living in a country of which they are not a citizen. (Pg 408)

5.   International Adjustment is:

    (a)   **the degree to which the expatriate feels comfortable living and working in the host culture. (Pg 409)**

    (b)   the amount of extra money the company has to pay to get a local manager to conform with head office requirements.

    (c)   the number of Host Country Nationals it takes to replace one Parent Country National.

    (d)   both (a) and (c).

6.   When expatriates undergo psychological uncertainty as a result of their experience in the host culture, they can be said to be going through:

    (a)   the culture consistency syndrome.

    (b)   culture shock. (Pg 410)

    (c)   a honeymoon period with their assignment.

    (d)   all of the above.

7.   The "adjustment" stage of the Culture Shock Cycle occurs:

    (a)   when the expatriate finally receives his/her foreign service premium.

    (b)   when the expatriate first encounters the new culture.

    (c)   as the expatriate begins to learns the norms of the new culture. (Pg 412)

    (d)   none of the above.

8.   The "mastery" stage of the Culture Shock Cycle indicates that the expatriate:

    (a)   is highly effective in, and enjoys the nuances of, the host culture.   (Pg 412)

    (b)   has "mastered" the skill of eating with chopsticks.

    (c)   has totally abandoned his/her original culture.

    (d)   both (a) and (c).

9.   Self-efficacy skills are important for the international manager because:

    (a)   they contribute to an ability to possess and retain a state of stable mental health.

    (b)   they add confidence to one's own ability to deal with unforeseen cross-cultural issues.

    (c)   they contribute to the person's technical competence.

    (d)   all of the above. (Pgs 415-416)

10.   "Conversational Currency" has to do with:

   (a)   the amount of fees lawyers charged for meeting with clients in different countries.
   (b)   tidbits of information about the local culture which can help make the expatriate more effective in interacting with host nationals. (Pg 418)
   (c)   the prevailing exchange rate of the US dollar in the black market, which is only given out verbally.
   (d)   both (b) and (c).

11.   The greater the novelty of the host culture,

   (a)   the more difficult it will be for the expatriate to adjust to that culture. (Pg 420)
   (b)   the higher they are on the scale of Individualism on Hofstede's dimensions.
   (c)   the more attractive it becomes for the expatriate.
   (d)   both (a) and (b).

12.   The greater the degree of role discretion,

   (a)   the better company secrets will be kept from competitors.
   (b)   the higher the level of conflict between the expatriate and the host nationals.
   (c)   the higher the level of adjustment the expatriate will experience on the job. (Pg 423)
   (d)   both (a) and (b).

13.   When selecting a candidate for overseas assignment, it is useful to:

   (a)   focus entirely on the person's past technical track record.
   (b)   include the person's spouse and family in the consideration. (Pg 425)
   (c)   ask the person to sign a contract saying he/she will stay.
   (d)   first ask the person's spouse to sign a contract saying he/she will stay.

14.   Relational skills can be evaluated through the use of:

   (a)   role playing.
   (b)   assessment centers.
   (c)   indepth interviews.
   (d)   all of the above. (Pg 427)

15.   Support systems that clarify work rules and procedure for the expatriates:

   (a)   should be paid for by the local subsidiary.
   (b)   should be standardized internationally for the whole company.
   (c)   are an integral part of the organizational culture dimension and help in the adjustment of the expatriate. (Pg 423)
   (d)   are usually specified by laws of the host country and are only instituted if local customs and laws require them.

B. True or False Questions

F (Pg 405)   1.   Parent Country Nationals are selected precisely because they are generally able to just step off the plane and perform well immediately.

F (Pg 406)   2. The biggest advantage of employing Host Country Nationals is that they are always paid much lower salaries.

T (Pg 407)   3.   Third Country Nationals tend to have already accumulated some international experience as well as foreign language skills from prior assignments.

F (Pg 408)   4. A Parent Country National, but not a Third Country National, can be considered an Expatriate.

T (Pg 410)   5. Expatriates generally will go through these stages of the Culture Shock Cycle: honeymoon, culture shock, adjustment, and mastery.

T (Pg 413)   6.   Anticipatory Socialization refers to people having anticipated the challenges of an overseas assignment and having begun to acculturate themselves before they leave home.

F (Pg 419)   7. Perception skills are not desirable in an international manager because we want him/her to be highly objective and not let perceptions get in the way of good judgement.

T (Pg 420)   8. Research has found that unless the expatriate's spouse and family also feel comfortable with the new culture, the expatriate will not perform at the desired level.

F (Pg 424)   9. Most companies take a multivariate approach to selecting candidates for overseas assignments, including testing for a variety of interpersonal and organizational skills.

T (Pg 428)   10. Countries that are quite dissimilar to North America would be considered high in culture novelty for North Americans.

C. Short Essay Questions

1. Compare and contrast the employment of Parent Country Nationals versus Host Country Nationals for subsidiary management positions.

Refer to Pgs 404-407.

2. Why is it important to consider the organizational culture of the subsidiary in selecting candidates for overseas assignments?

Refer to Pgs 423-424.

3. What role does relational skills play in determining how well a person will adjust internationally? Why?

Refer to Pgs 416-418.

Chapter 13

Training for International Assignments

Chapter Summary:

Most US firms do not train their expatriates before they send them overseas. This chapter examines the need for cross-cultural training, and contrasts this need with the lack of interest exhibited by many US-based firms. Because research has demonstrated the usefulness of cross-cultural training, several approaches to training are introduced in this chapter. These different approaches include the more common type of information or fact-oriented training, and extend to experiential training which aims to instill a sense of the real nature of life in another culture in the employee. Different techniques can be used to implement training, and some unusual ones are highlighted in the chapter. Exhibit 13.2 (Pg 445), for instance, gives a summary of what a "cultural assimilator" may look like.

Training methods vary from relatively low-rigor approaches such as area briefings to those that are very rigorous, such as simulations. The human resource manager needs to assess the level of rigor that is required, and three important variables should be considered--job novelty, degree of interaction with host nationals, and culture novelty. These variables are discussed at length in the chapter.

Three conceptual models of training method selection are introduced in the chapter, each building on the previous one. The Black and Mendenhall model (see Pg 452) is based on social learning theory, and provides a useful framework (both conceptually and in practice) for the manager in choosing the appropriate training method. Exhibit 13.5 (Pg 452) and Exhibit 13.6 (Pg 453) taken together provide a easy-to-use decision tree for the practicing manager. In essence, the greater the culture novelty, required degree of interaction with host nationals, and job novelty, the greater the need for rigorous cross-cultural training.

The importance of cross-cultural training is illustrated by many case examples, and it would be an interesting class exercise for students to find more such examples from doing some library work (see below).

Suggested Class Agenda:

The decision tree as proposed by the Black and Mendenhall model should be a chief area of learning in this session. Exhibits 13.5 and 13.6 are critical aspects of the chapter for students to master. We suggest that at least half the session be devoted to a detailed discussion of this part, in which case students can be encouraged to contribute to the dialogue by doing some prior library research on the actual training practices of multinationals.

The case examples of failures due to insufficient cross-cultural training (Pgs 457-458) can be augmented with more examples, either provided by the instructor or researched by students themselves. The business press reports a large variety of such mistakes, and a brief trip to the library should yield fruitful results.

For more involved classroom discussions, Discussion Question (3) can be a pre-assigned task for students (perhaps in groups) and the results of their analysis reported in this session. This would be a useful way to end the session.

Overheads:

#1   Training Method Selection

        Exhibit #13.5   Page 452

#2   Training Scenarios

        Exhibit #13.6   Page 453

#3   Training Rigor

        Exhibit #13.3   Page 447

Discussion Questions:

1.   Many firms do not advocate training for international assignments because of the time and expense involved. Evaluate this approach.

     refer to Pgs 440-442.

2.   Assume you are human resource manager of a Canadian firm arranging the transfer of an Australian manager to the US. Discuss the need for training for this assignment.

     The more involved student would point out that there are three main cultures involved here, each with its idiosyncrasies, despite a common (?) language in general. As a result, some discussion of the cultural diversity involved in this situation is warranted. As for the need for training, refer to Pg 440 and Pgs 457-459 for more ideas. Students may want to supplement their comments with case examples that they manage to find, and this should be a welcomed contribution.

3.   Assume that you have been assigned to a post in a foreign country that you believe is culturally very different from your home country. Your firm does not typically provide indepth training for such assignments. Prepare an argument to present to your boss outlining what training you feel is appropriate and explaining why this is needed.

     Some assumptions will need to be made as to the nature of the job, the different countries of interest, the nature of the person involved, and so on. Having done that, it would be useful to refer to Exhibits 13.5 and 13.6 for a guideline. The importance of cross-cultural training is highlighted in some detail in the chapter, particularly Pgs 457-458. How well the arguments are formulated of course also depends a lot on the student's persuasion skills.

Test Questions:

A. Multiple Choice Questions

1. A key assumption behind cross-cultural training programs is that:

    (a)   an expatriate will better adjust to the new culture.
    (b)   an expatriate will become more satisfied with the assignment.
    (c)   an expatriate will become more effective on the new job.
    (d)   all of the above. (Pg 440)

2. The main reason why many companies do not offer cross-cultural training is that:

    (a)   they do not think the training is effective. (Pgs 440-441)
    (b)   they are purely domestic companies.
    (c)   foreign governments see cross-cultural training as another example of American imperialism.
    (d)   culture has no place in the business world.

3. Attribution Training is aimed at:

    (a)   providing the employee with a factual rundown of the attributes of host nationals.
    (b)   helping employees better understand the behavior of host nationals. (Pg 443)
    (c)   helping employees to deal with psychological distress by attributing their negative feelings to environmental factors.
    (d)   changing the employee's attitudes towards the training program.

4. The training method which requires trainees to practice their cross-cultural skills in hypothetical situations is called:

    (a)   experiential training. (Pg 443)
    (b)   cultural awareness training.
    (c)   self-hypnosis training.
    (d)   sensitivity training.

5.   Simulations are highly complex role plays which few businesses have used. The reason is that:

        (a)   the Peace Corps has found them ineffective.
        (b)   very powerful computers are needed before the simulations can begin.
        (c)   this type of training is very costly both in terms of time and money. (Pg 446)
        (d)   none of the above.

6.   Three important variables determine the level of rigor required in cross-cultural training. They are:

        (a)   job novelty, degree of interaction with host nationals, and culture novelty. (Pgs 448-449)
        (b)   time, money, and top management country of origin.
        (c)   job novelty, budget availability, and the country of the company's head office.
        (d)   degree of interaction with head office, culture novelty, and job security.

7.   Samantha, the company's tax accountant from Detroit, will be taking over as public relations director of the firm's subsidiary in Malaysia. Which of the following training program would seem most appropriate?

        (a)   lecture, films, books.
        (b)   lecture, factual briefing, cases.
        (c)   culture assimilator, books, role play.
        (d)   both (b) and (c). (Pg 453)

8.   Research has shown that adjusting to the host culture

        (a)   and interacting with host nationals are more difficult tasks than adjusting to the overseas job. (Pg 452)
        (b)   is nowhere near as difficult as adjusting to the new job.
        (c)   is about as difficult as interacting with host nationals, but easier than dealing with a new job assignment.
        (d)   is a non-issue in the business world because decisions should be made on a purely economic basis.

9.   Culture novelty has to do with:

   (a)   how recent a particular culture came into being.
   **(b)   the notion that some cultures are more similar in terms of their value
            systems, behavioral norms, and so on. (Pg 449)**
   (c)   the idea that the newer a particular culture is, the more novelty it has, and
           thus the easier it is to acculturate.
   (d)   all of the above.

10.   In assessing the degree of interaction with host nationals, it is useful to consider:

   (a)   the choice of training programs.
   (b)   how novel the nature of the job is.
   (c)   how important are the interactions to the subsidiary's success. (Pg 449)
   (d)   from which university the degree is obtained.

11.   In general, it is best in cross-cultural training to:

   (a)   use as much simulation and experiential training as possible.
   (b)   use a combination of methods. (Pg 456)
   (c)   hire outside consultants.
   (d)   give the employee a bonus for attending the training.

12.   Some cross-cultural trainers have argued that it is more effective to offer more-
        rigorous training methods to expatriates *after* they have been overseas and have
        gained some experience in the host culture. The rationale is that:

   (a)   time will not allow a full training regiment prior to departure.
   (b)   the expatriate will be too anxious prior to departure to want to learn
           anything.
   (c)   companies want to make sure the expatriate will stay in the new job before
           paying for the training.
   **(d)   it is difficult for the expatriate to envision complex cross-cultural
            situations without some actual experience with the new culture. (Pg 456)**

13.   The rigor of a cross-cultural training program refers to:

    (a)   how physically demanding it is.

    (b)   how much the trainee has to exert cognitive, behavioral, and emotional effort. (Pg 448)

    (c)   how long the program takes and how many people participate at one time.

    (d)   the level of the trainee in the organization's hierarchy.

14.   Sensitivity Training is not much used by corporations because:

    (a)   it generally requires a lot of time away from work. (Pg 446)

    (b)   it is not rigorous enough for most cross cultural situations.

    (c)   it does not work in a business environment.

    (d)   businesses do not want sensitive managers, they want tough minds.

15.   Which of the following combination of cross-cultural training methods is arranged in ascending order of training rigor?

    (a)   books, field trips, sensitivity training.

    (b)   lectures, role plays, films.

    (c)   area briefings, sensitivity training, field trips. (Pg 447)

    (d)   culture assimilators, lectures, books.

B. True or False Questions

T (Pg 440)   1. Some 65% of US firms do not offer any kind of training to their expatriates before sending them overseas.

F (Pg 443)   2. Cultural Awareness training is the most commonly used cross-cultural training method in business.

F (Pg 444)   3. Culture Assimilator refers to how well an employee has assimilated into the new culture.

T (Pg 447)   4. Cross-cultural training programs that are high in rigor often entail a high level of participation by the trainees.

F (Pg 448)   5. Job novelty is the most important variable affecting decisions on the level of training rigor required.

F (Pg 449)   6. Culture novelty refers to how new the host society's culture is.

T (Pg 449)   7. All things being equal, the higher the level of culture novelty, the more rigorous the training needs to be.

T (Pg 451)   8. Immersion approaches to cross-cultural training are high in rigor and trainee participation.

F (Pg 455)   9. US firms commonly provide cross-cultural training to the expatriate and his/her family members.

F (Pg 457)   10. Cross-cultural training is really only necessary for long term assignments overseas.

C. Short Essay Questions

1. What are the general approaches to cross-cultural training and how do they differ?

   refer to Pg 443.

2. Discuss how a "culture assimilator" works.

   refer to Pg 444 and Exhibit 13.2

3. What are the three important variables to consider in determining the level of rigor required in cross-cultural training? Discuss how these variables interact to affect the level of rigor necessary.

   refer to Pgs 448-449, and Pg 452, as well as Exhibits 13.5 and 13.6.

Chapter 14

Managing the Expatriate Manager

Chapter Summary:

One of the key issues to understand about expatriates is the paradoxes they face in their new positions overseas--particularly in regards to their sense of allegiance and the way in which they deal with uncertainty of their role in the overseas environment. At a minimum, human resource executives need to understand these challenges and construct organizational mechanisms that will assist expatriates to avoid or overcome them. This chapter begins with an examination of four common paradoxes that confront the expatriate--the dual loyalty paradox, the unlearned expert paradox, the identification/acculturation paradox, and the believing yet disbelieving in stereotypes paradox. Each of these paradoxes is worthy of some discussion in class.

Some organizational mechanisms which can help in overcoming these paradoxes are introduced in the chapter, and these include overseas support systems, integration programs, and mentor programs. In addition, the human resource manager has to pay attention to the design and implementation of performance appraisals for expatriates, which are often a major problem in view of the lack of clearcut delineation of where the responsibility for appraisal lies.

Compensation for expatriates is another important topic that the chapter discusses. In particular, commonly used terms describing various components of an expatriate's compensation are studied, to provide the reader with the necessary knowledge to address this very important issue.

The task of a human resource executive in managing an expatriate workforce does not end with compensation. Indeed, upon repatriation, more problems arise. The chapter closes out with a detailed discussion of the issues associated with repatriation, and how repatriation adjustments can be dealt with.

Suggested Class Agenda:

The class can be split into four small groups, each assigned the task of digesting and reflecting on one of the four paradoxes outlined in the chapter. Each group, after some time to analyze the issues, then presents to the rest of the class its understanding and reflections on the assigned paradox. This should be a fruitful exercise, designed not only to make students carefully consider the implications of each of the paradoxes, but also to "warm up" the students for a more interactive class discussion of the repatriation problem in the latter part of the session.

A brief lecture on the various organizational mechanisms to combat the paradoxes would be of value, especially if students (now that they are "warmed up") are encouraged to voice their studied opinions as to the efficacy of each. The section on compensation should not require the instructor to spend much time lecturing.

We would recommend that a considerable amount of time be spent on repatriation, since this is a commonly overlooked area. Here, Exhibit 14.3 (Pg 489) would be a useful visual cue. Students should by now be quite familiar with most of the terms here, and should be encouraged to participate actively in a discussion. For more involved classes, students can be asked beforehand to do some secondary research into repatriation problems, and to present case examples reported in the business press to supplement the text.

Overheads:

#1   The Dual Loyalty Paradox

Exhibit 14.1, Pg 468.

#2   The Believing, Yet Disbelieving in Stereotypes Paradox

Exhibit 14.2, Pg 475.

#3   Fighting the Paradoxes

Overseas Support Systems
Integration Programs
Mentor Programs

#4   Overseas Performance Appraisals

> *Factors of success for overseas operations*
> *Input from the expatriate*
> *On-site manager and former expatriate to evaluate*

#5   Repatriation Problems

> *Exhibit 14.3, Pg 489*

Discussion Questions:

1.   As a manager born in India, educated in the United Kingdom, and currently working for a US-headquartered firm in its Canadian subsidiary, identify the loyalty conflicts that you would likely encounter.

   This is an interesting but very common phenomenon. Students should make use of the discussion of the Dual Loyalty Paradox on Pgs 467-471.

2.   Identify and discuss the kinds of expertise that a parent country national (PCN) is likely to have that makes it appropriate to send them on foreign assignments.

   Students will need to carefully examine the discussion of the four paradoxes to fully appreciate the scope of this question. Furthermore, attention should also paid to issues raised in earlier chapters, specifically Chapter 12.

3.   Discuss the advantages and disadvantages of compensating an expatriate, working outside of the parent country, on the basis of prevailing compensation systems in the parent country.

   refer to Pgs 484-486.

Test Questions:

A. Multiple Choice Questions

1.   Human resource executives are often of little help to the expatriate in overcoming the challenges of working and living in a new culture because:

    (a)   the human resource executive may themselves be expatriates facing the same challenges.

    (b)   the human resource executive may be stationed at head office and thus too far away to actually be of help.

    (c)   the human resource executive may not have the budget or staff to render the necessary assistance.

    (d)   all of the above. (Pgs 466-467)

2.   The Dual Loyalty Paradox refers to:

    (a)   an expatriate torn between his/her loyalty to head office and to the subsidiary/host country. (Pgs 467-468)

    (b)   citizenship problems that expatriates face because local governments often require expatriates to renounce their original citizenship.

    (c)   acculturation problems facing an expatriate after a prolonged engagement in a new culture.

    (d)   expatriates who quit their jobs and become unemployed in a new country.

3.   Expatriates who have "gone native" are those who:

    (a)   become citizens of the host society and never return to their original countries.

    (b)   learn to fluently speak and write the local language.

    (c)   have high levels of allegiance to the local operation but low levels of allegiance to the home office. (Pg 469)

    (d)   leave the MNC and join the operations of a locally-owned competitor.

4.   Expatriates who are "dual citizens" have:

    (a)   passports from both the home and host countries.

    (b)   a high level of loyalty to both the parent firm and the local operation. (Pg 470)

    (c)   should be terminated at once.

    (d)   are destined to "go native."

5.   An expatriate who constantly assumes the role of an expert

      (a)   should be given increasing levels of authority.
      (b)   engenders cooperation among the local staff.
      (c)   runs the risk of making serious blunders by being too self-confident. (Pg 472)
      (d)   suffers from an acute case of the "unlearned expert" paradox.

6.   An individual who possesses superior cross-cultural skills will be committed to seeing the essential similarities between people from different cultures

      (a)   while maintaining an equally strong commitment to valuing their differences. (Pg 474)
      (b)   and treat everybody the same way so as to be fair.
      (c)   and abhor the formation of any sort of stereotypes.
      (d)   while encouraging the local staff to become more modernized.

7.   A well-designed integration program should:

      (a)   focus solely on shopping and dining attractions for the newly arrived expatriate.
      (b)   be centrally managed from head office.
      (c)   provide opportunities for expatriates to merge into the local culture. (Pg 478)
      (d)   both (b) and (c).

8.   Mentor programs can serve to give the expatriate:

      (a)   a formalized link back to the home office and a host-national mentor to help them understand the workings of the local business culture. (Pg 479)
      (b)   a chance to go back to school to upgrade their skills.
      (c)   the opportunity to become human resource planners.
      (d)   all of the above.

9.   A critical issue in measuring an expatriate's performance is:

      (a)   job novelty.
      (b)   whether the expatriate is a PCN or a TCN.
      (c)   whether the host national or the home office does the measuring. (Pg 481)
      (d)   how much to pay the expatriate for his/her foreign service.

10. Doing an indepth study of what the key factors of success are for the overseas operation has the advantage of:

   (a)   overcoming the dual loyalty paradox.
   (b)   providing the basis for more effective performance appraisals. (Pg 483)
   (c)   avoiding repatriation problems.
   (d)   reducing the amount of salaries paid to expatriates.

11. A Foreign Service Premium refers to:

   (a)   an increase in insurance premiums because the person is working overseas.
   (b)   what the State Department routinely pays out in foreign service subsidies to expatriates.
   (c)   extra pay that companies provide to expatriates for working outside their home country. (Pg 485)
   (d)   an award for providing excellent customer service in a foreign country.

12. Repatriation means:

   (a)   returning to one's own country. (Pg 486)
   (b)   being sent on a second overseas assignment.
   (c)   the problems of adjustment after being sent overseas.
   (d)   the recurring problems of dual loyalty after two years overseas.

13. When compared to the repatriates' overseas positions, their new home positions tend to have:

   (a)   less autonomy and authority.
   (b)   less responsibility.
   (c)   are usually lateral career moves.
   (d)   all of the above. (Pg 488)

14. Looking back on their overseas assignments, the vast majority of repatriates:

   (a)   did not think it had been helpful to their careers. (Pg 488)
   (b)   did think it had been helpful to their careers.
   (c)   wish they had not repatriated their funds.
   (d)   felt sorry for having "gone native."

15.   A major problem in repatriation adjustment is:

   (a)   the cost of airline tickets.
   (b)   language barrier.
   (c)   foreign government refusing to give exit visas.
   (d)   inaccurate expectations about what life will be like. (Pg 491)

B. True or False Questions

F (Pg 465)   1. The firm's responsibility to the expatriate's adjustment process ends once cross-training has been completed.

T (Pg 467)   2. A human resource executive who has an indepth knowledge of the challenges facing an expatriate can be helpful to the expatriate's adjustment.

F (Pg 467)   3. Dual Loyalty is a phenomenon that happens only when US nationals are sent to Japan.

F (Pg 468)   4. An expatriate who has low allegiance to both the parent firm and the local operation is a "dual citizen."

T (Pg 477)   5. Good knowledge of the host country and good interpersonal skills are important prerequisites for the family coordinator.

F (Pg 484)   6. In expatriate compensation, a "base salary" refers to a minimum-wage pay level which is supplemented with commissions based on sales.

F (Pg 485)   7. "COLA" is a commonly used term in expatriate compensation meaning an increase in pay to the next salary range.

T (Pg 486)   8. Often, what expatriates think will happen to them when they get home and what actually takes place are quite different.

T (Pg 488)   9. Most US firms do not seem to place much emphasis on an employee's experience as an expatriate.

T (Pg 493)   10. Some 70% of Japanese expatriates feel a major loss in quality of life upon repatriation.

C. Short Essay Questions

1. Why would an "unlearned expert" be more productive in overseas assignments?

    refer to Pg 472.

2. Discuss why repatriates may have inaccurate expectations about what life will be like after returning home?

    refer to Pg 487.

3. What can companies do organizationally to help the repatriate cope with adjustment?

    refer to Pgs 490-491.

Chapter 15

Special Issues for Global Firm: Women and Dual-Career Couples

Chapter Summary:

Increasingly, the world of international management is not the sole purview of men. Women managers represent an important pool of talent that an international firm would be obtuse to ignore. Related to this, but significant in its own right, is the question of dual-career couples. The human resource executive has to understand the unique problems that confront women expatriates and dual-career couples.

The role of women in different parts of the world is examined in this chapter, and real examples are used to illustrate the diversity of social norms and cultural values that affect women. Students should gain some insights as to the difficulties that not only the firm, but also the women themselves face when placing women expatriates in certain foreign countries. The subject of ethnocentrism is given some discussion, and students should come away with a sense that one cannot really "judge" another society's social values based solely on what is "right or wrong" at home.

Dual-career couples pose their own blend of problems when planning for expatriate assignments. These are discussed in detail in the chapter. Suggestions are made (Pgs 523-525) for companies to deal productively with the matter; dual-career couples can bring significant contributions to an international firm if planned for/catered to accordingly.

Suggested Class Agenda:

There are several very interesting exercises that the students can be asked to undertake, so as to reinforce the lessons from this session and also to move the students to reflect on what they have learned. Each of these exercises requires some amount of pre-session work.

Ask students to contact the embassies, consulates, trade commissions, etc. of a number of foreign countries, to find out the legal restrictions pertaining to dual-career couples. Specifically, what are the laws governing an expatriate executive's spouse who may want to seek employment in that country? For example, are visas and work permits granted? How? This exercise is aimed at providing some solid information from which the plight of the dual-career couple can be examined in class.

Another exercise involves doing some secondary research to answer Discussion Question (1). This should lead to an interesting class discussion, depending on how much students are able to find from the literature. We would suggest that the more senior the class, and commensurate with the more experience they have in doing secondary research, the more fruitful this exercise will be.

Students can also be asked to talk to exchange students from other countries to seek the latter's views on the role of women in their own countries. In addition, students can be asked to talk to both males and females from each country, so that a "balanced" viewpoint is obtained. This should supplement the text quite well.

Lecture points can focus on several key topics in the chapter. A particularly useful topic would be the different perspectives on "equality." People can be talking about different things though the same term is used. It is important that students be aware of this possible discrepancy. In addition, students may wish to bring in their own interpretations of what equality means.

Another useful lecture topic would be plight of the dual-career couple, and especially those where the wife is the expatriate executive. Related to this would be the proactive approaches that an organization can take, not only in behalf of these couples, but also to actually benefit from this enlarged pool of talent.

Overheads:

    #1   Meaning of Equality

        A. Standardized, equitable treatment regardless of gender.

        B. Differences exist, equitable treatment based on different contributions.

        What do YOU think?

    #2   Shortage of Women in Top Management

        *past discrimination
        *present discrimination
        *lack of interest
        *lack of education and training

Discussion Questions:

1. Identify recent trends regarding women in management in your home country and discuss how this is likely to influence firms from that country sending managers on foreign assignments.

    To fully (and intelligently) answer this question, students ought to do some secondary research to determine "recent trends" and not simply base their discussions on their own personal perceptions. The second part of this question can conceptually benefit from a review of Pgs 514-517.

2. Discuss the unique challenges that may be faced by male spouses of expatriates and suggest ways of managing these challenges.

    Refer to Pgs 521-525.

3. Discuss the impact of the changing role of women in North American firms on international staffing decisions by North American firms.

    refer to Pg 514.

Test Questions:

A. Multiple Choice Questions

1.   Ethnocentrism is a common phenomenon having to do with the fact that:

     **(a)   people often find it difficult to accept values and norms that differ from
            what is considered acceptable in their home countries. (Pg 502)**
     (b)   ethnic groups are centralized in their organization.
     (c)   people from different cultures tend to socialize with "their own kind" for
            reasons of language and taste differences.
     (d)   many people value their ethnic origins much more so than their country of
            citizenship.

2.   The United Nations reported that the employment of women in developing
     countries by international firms:

     (a)   unequivocally exploit these women, and urged member nations to pass
            legislation protecting the rights of these women.
     (b)   represents a large portion of the international firm's worldwide
            employment.
     (c)   is only about 3 percent of these firm's total workforce. (Pg 503)
     (d)   represents a significant proportion of the total labor force of these countries.

3.   The balance between exploitation and providing employment for women workers
     is:

     (a)   well-delineated by law.
     (b)   one of little significance in foreign countries.
     (c)   is dependent solely on how much the women workers are paid.
     (d)   is a fine-line which is not always clear-cut. (Pg 504)

4.   Which of the following unequivocally indicates the speaker's disregard for sexual
     equality?

     (a)   women and men are equal in all respects and should be treated the same
            way.
     (b)   men and women *are* different, and ignoring the differences does not make
            the best use of the varying abilities and interests of the sexes.
     **(c)   women and men are different, and equality only makes sense *within* each
            sex and not *across* sexes. (Pg 507)**
     (d)   none of the above.

5.   Legal provisions in some countries:

(a)   may make it very onerous for local women to function effectively as managers.

(b)   may require women to retire earlier than men.

(c)   may allow women to work only if their husbands cannot financially support the family.

(d)   all of the above. (Pg 501, 508)

6.   Which of the following is perhaps **not** a cause of the lack of women in top management ranks?

(a)   women are too "soft" and not strong-minded enough. (Pg 509)

(b)   ongoing discrimination against women.

(c)   some women are not interested.

(d)   a shortage of women with appropriate education and training.

7.   Compared to Canada and the US, European women are:

(a)   much better-represented in management ranks.

(b)   not as well represented in management ranks. (Pg 511)

(c)   much more educated.

(d)   much less educated.

8.   There will be more women international managers because:

(a)   there is an increasing number of women domestic managers.

(b)   more women are eager to take on overseas assignments.

(c)   both (a) and (b). (Pg 514)

(d)   neither (a) nor (b).

9.   Research has shown that women make good expatriate managers:

(a)   even in locations where local women would generally not be well-accepted as managers. (Pg 515)

(b)   only if the host country is open to having women as managers.

(c)   even in locations where local women are not accepted as managers but only if they manage other women.

(d)   only if they work for a US international firm.

10.   If the international firm abides by local legislations which govern the kind of jobs and roles that women can take,

    (a)   then it is on safe legal grounds in terms of sexual equality.

    (b)   it can still be breaking the law at home in terms of sexual equality. (Pg 517)

    (c)   it should change its internal policies to standardize this practice.

    (d)   both (a) and (c).

11.   Companies that believe the problems associated with the relocation of spouses in dual-career couples are a family or personal matter:

    (a)   run the risk of being sued by the employee and his/her spouse.

    (b)   are being smart not to get involved in an employee's private matters.

    (c)   may be limiting their pool of candidates for overseas assignments. (Pg 518)

    (d)   should have hired both spouses instead.

12.   The spouse of an expatriate in a dual-career couple may suffer career sacrifices because:

    (a)   some host countries will not give work permits to spouses.

    (b)   it may be culturally unacceptable for women to work in that society.

    (c)   professional requirements and designations may not be transferrable across national borders.

    (d)   all of the above. (Pg 522)

13.   One of the ways an international firm can alleviate some of the concerns of the dual-career couple moving to another country is:

    (a)   consider opportunities for job sharing if both spouses are in the same field.

    (b)   provide more time for the move.

    (c)   consider and help with reentry problems.

    (d)   all of the above. (Pgs 523-524)

14.   Realistic predeparture information on foreign job opportunities are:

    (a)   very helpful for the dual-career couple. (Pg 523)

    (b)   dangerous because they invariably lead to the expatriate quitting.

    (c)   impossible to get because of geographic distances.

    (d)   both (a) and (c).

15.   Firms that respect the concerns of dual-career couples may:

    (a)   be boycotted by cultural activists.
    (b)   benefit from a better ability to motivate, attract, and retain employees. (Pg 525)
    (c)   find themselves the subject of lawsuits by foreign governments.
    (d)   unknowingly exploit the spouse of the expatriate.

B. True or False Questions

T (Pg 502)   1.   In considering employing women workers overseas, differential treatment of women can be seen as protection or discrimination.

F (Pg 507)   2.   Sexual equality has clear-cut meanings and is not subject to misunderstandings.

F (Pg 503)   3.   International firms are responsible for the employment of most of the developing countries' women workers.

T (Pg 504)   4.   One of the dilemmas facing an international manager is that the distinction between providing employment and exploiting women workers is not always clear-cut.

F (Pg 505)   5. European countries invariably give more equal treatment to women workers than in North America.

T (Pg 511)   6.   North American firms tend to have more women managers than their European counterparts.

T (Pg 513)   7.   In China, most top management positions are filled by men.

T (Pg 515)   8.   North American women managers in Japan are viewed as "foreigner" rather than as "women" and their gender is not an impediment to competent management.

T (Pg 517)   9.   Some foreign countries have laws detailing the role and position of women.

F (Pg 521)   10.   The dual-career couple problem is simplified if the situation is one of a woman expatriate and a male spouse.

C. Short Essay Questions

1.   Discuss the meaning of gender equality. What are the two major alternative views?

        refer to Pg 507.

2.   What are some reasons for a lack of women in top management positions in North America?

        refer to Pg 509.

3.   Why should companies be concerned with the problems of relocating dual-career couples? What are some things companies can do to help alleviate the problem?

        refer to Pg 518, and to Pgs 523-524.

Chapter 16

Communication and Negotiation in Global Management

Chapter Summary:

This chapter reviews the important aspects of cross-cultural communications in order to better prepare the students for working with people from other cultures. Five fundamental dimensions of human communications are discussed, with concrete examples illustrating how problems may surface under each of the dimensions. The upshot is that to communicate effectively with others from a different culture, one must first learn not only the language, but also the rules for how the language is used in different contexts and situations, and this includes nonverbal behavior.

Several barriers exist to block effective communication, and these must be understood and surmounted. Each of these barriers is examined in detail, and suggestions are made to enable students to try to overcome them.

In the business setting, negotiations often are one of the most important aspects of cross-cultural communications. It has been found that in general people from all cultures go through four stages in the negotiation process--relationship building, exchange of task-related information, persuasion, and making concessions and agreement. The important point to note, however, is that the degree to which value is placed on each stage differs across cultures. The negotiation styles of several societies--i.e. Brazil, China, and Russia-- are highlighted to illustrate their differences.

Suggested Agenda:

A meaningful exercise for student involvement is to split the class into five smaller groups, each charged with reviewing one of the five fundamental dimensions of communications and to come up with examples to illustrate the dimension. This adds to the text discussion and allows students to better internalize the knowledge.

If there are foreign students in the class, their perspectives of the communication process at work in their home countries can add to the value of the session. Alternatively, students can be asked to interview one or two foreign students outside this class to get their perspectives.

A general discussion of Discussion Question (2) should raise the level of consciousness among the students as to communications characteristics within their own society.

Depending on the level of the class, a brief lecture on the five fundamental dimensions may be called for. Regardless of level, it may be a good idea to offer a quick lecture on the important topic of barriers to communications, especially in the context of cross-cultural communications. The four stages of the negotiation process is another useful lecture point, though the instructor may also wish to ask students (or volunteers) to lead discussion on them.

Overheads:

#1   Five dimensions of Communications

Communication is a Process
Purposive vs Expressive Messages
Multi-Unit Signals
Context
Competence

#2   High and Low Context Cultures

High Context: culturally homogeneous

Low Context: culturally heterogeneous

#3   Communication Barriers

Ignorance of Cultural Rules
Perceptual Biases
Faulty Attributions
Stereotypes

#4   Negotiation: 4 stages

Relationship Building
Exchange Information
Persuasion
Concessions and Agreement

Discussion Questions:

1.   Discuss how "noise" is likely to enter the communication process when Japanese managers talk to their US counterparts.

Conceptually, it is important that the five dimensions of communication and the barriers are examined. To this end, students should be familiar with the material covered in Pgs 535-550. In terms of specifics regarding Japan-US communications, examples abound throughout the chapter, and students should have little trouble coming up with examples.

2.   Identify specific non-verbal aspects of communications that are important in communicating in your home country. Discuss how these non-verbal activities influence communication effectiveness.

This is a very good question for general class discussion. For conceptual discussions on non-verbal communications, students should refer to Pgs 539-550.

3.   Discuss your home country and a contrasting country in terms of their approach to the various stages of communication.

Answers vary, but attention should be paid to the five dimensions highlighted in the chapter (Pgs 535-539).

Test Questions:

A. Multiple Choice Questions

1.   Because communication is a process, it is an ongoing exchange of messages and:

    (a)   one never knows when the other has stopped talking.
    (b)   there must be some economic value attached to the exchange.
    (c)   content is secondary.
    (d)   communication relationships affect what is communicated. (Pg 535)

2.   Expressive messages are those that:

    (a)   are unintentionally sent along with a spoken message. (Pg 536)
    (b)   express a general idea but with little purpose in mind.
    (c)   use a lot of adjectives to express an idea.
    (d)   are sent quickly so as to avoid ambiguity.

3.   Communication is highly dependent on the "context" for its meanings, in which case:

    (a)   one should always ask the other part what the context is.
    (b)   high-context cultures generally rely more on non-verbal communications. (Pg 538)
    (c)   low-context cultures generally cannot be well understood.
    (d)   both (b) and (c).

4.   Competence of the communicator refers to:

    (a)   how well the communicator knows the language and the rules governing its use. (Pg 539)
    (b)   the number of degrees in communication the person holds.
    (c)   how many languages the person speaks.
    (d)   whether the person has good friends in the host country.

5.   Kinesics refers to:

(a)   the study of energy and motion.
(b)   verbal expressions in a foreign country.
(c)   gestures, facial expressions, and other non-verbal communication.   (Pg 540)
(d)   spatial relationships in human communication.

6.   In Japan, the size of a person's office:

(a)   may have little to do with the person's importance. (Pg 541)
(b)   is a good indicator of the person's importance.
(c)   depends on the person's age.
(d)   is generally related to the size of the company.

7.   In high-context cultures, privacy:

(a)   is highly valued because of the context.
(b)   may not be very important in the workplace. (Pg 542)
(c)   is only available for important people.
(d)   is important only in the workplace.

8.   Mental categories refer to:

(a)   whether the person is visually or verbally oriented.
(b)   the way a person sees his/her personal space.
(c)   the way people simplify the world around them and store information. (Pg 544)
(d)   whether one is externally or internally attributive.

9.   Internal attributions are made when behavior is seen as:

(a)   caused by domestic political pressures.
(b)   caused by the person's internal characteristics. (Pg 549)
(c)   a reaction to the internal operations of the organization.
(d)   a result of one's inability to blame others for mistakes.

10.   To make correct attributions cross-culturally, it is important to:

(a)   put one's attributions "on hold." (Pg 550)
(b)   make both internal and external attributions at the same time.
(c)   rely only on external attributions.
(d)   rely only on internal attributions.

11.   When a person categorizes a group of people based on some features that they hold in common, such as nationality, race, or religion, this person is:

(a)   not a good candidate for overseas assignments.
(b)   a racist.
(c)   stereotyping. (Pg 550)
(d)   attributing externally.

12.   Which of the following statement is not true?

(a)   relationship building is practiced by all cultures in negotiations.
(b)   when negotiating with the Japanese, one should make a lot of small concessions along the way. (Pg 553)
(c)   Americans tend to rely on logic and rationality in their negotiations and tend to suppress the need for interpersonal relationships.
(d)   both the Japanese and the Americans see persuasion as an important step in negotiations.

13.   The "linking" approach to a "receptive" style of influence involves:

(a)   a desire to win over the opponent by ingratiating oneself to the other party.
(b)   an attempt to better understand and empathize with the other party. (Pg 554)
(c)   joining forces with other third parties so as to achieve a better bargaining position.
(d)   appealing to the other party's common sense.

14.   Holistic thinking affects the negotiation process because:

(a)   Americans tend to practice it more often.

(b)   concessions are made throughout the negotiating process.

(c)   little progress will be made until the party can see how the big picture will unfold. (Pg 557)

(d)   concessions are used as tradeoffs and must be reciprocated.

15.   In negotiations, Brazilians, as compared to Japanese and Americans, tend to:

(a)   be more aggressive and vocal in their demands.

(b)   avoid confrontation at all cost.

(c)   use more linking but less seducing approaches.

(d)   use the "receptive" approach. (Pg 554)

B. True or False Questions

T (Pg 536)   1. Purposive messages are those that are sent intentionally.

T (Pg 536)   2. Nonverbal messages are just as important as verbal communication.

F (Pg 536)   3. The "context" of communication refers to how often the parties come into bodily contact, and is a measure of spatial relationships.

T (Pg 540)   4. It is inappropriate to point the soles of one's shoes toward the host in Indonesia.

T (Pg 545)   5. People from different cultures process and categorize information differently.

T (Pg 550)   6. In-group heterogeneity and out-group homogeneity is a manifestation of stereotyping.

F (Pg 551)   7. The amount of time that is spent on each stage of the negotiation process has nothing to do with the importance that is attached to each of the stages.

T (Pg 553)   8. Americans tend to see an exchange of task-related information as less important than Japanese do.

F (Pg 553)   9. It is because of holistic thinking that American negotiators tend to make a series of small concessions along the way.

F (Pg 556)   10. The Chinese practice of seeking an agreement on "general principles" when engaging in negotiations is only rhetoric, and has little relationship with what they are really after.

C. Short Essay Questions

1.   How does one go about achieving competence in communication?

   refer to Pg 538.

2.   Discuss the concept of "semifixed features of space," and comment on how they affect cross-cultural communications.

   refer to Pg 542.

3.   How does the notion of faulty attributions come into play in cross-cultural negotiations?

   refer to Pgs 546-550, but care should be paid to the need to also focus on "negotiations" rather than simply communications.

Chapter 17

Leadership and Motivation in a Global Context

Chapter Summary:

Motivating and leading people from cultural backgrounds other than one's own is a valuable skill that the international manager needs to master. This chapter reviews the important principles associated with leading and motivating people in a cross-cultural context.

Leaders tend to have a vision, even an obsession, and they are able to inspire others to follow them in a focused pursuit of this vision. But apart from this general observation, leadership does not consist of one set of universal laws but is a quality that must be exercised in the context of the culture in which the manager operates. The chapter provides various examples of where "good" leadership in one society may be seen as "bad" in another.

Various theories have been offered on leaders and motivation, and some of the prominent ones are discussed in this chapter. These theories are primarily developed out of a Western perspective, and their applicability across national and cultural boundaries may be in doubt. As a result, the chapter also spends considerable time analyzing research findings pertaining to the global application of some of these theories. As things stand, no one theory stands out as warranting unrestricted use by people cross-culturally. On the other hand, the expectancy theory offers a potential of wide applicability, if the manager understands the needs of his/her subordinates.

Suggested Class Agenda:

The instructor may wish to consider the structure of this session as a "balancing act." On the one hand, the chapter is imbued with numerous examples borrowed from real life, so students get a vivid illustration of the life of an expatriate in a foreign land.(And many students will find this of immense value.) On the other hand, some students may desire a concrete "now what?" kind of pedagogy, in which case we can anticipate questions like "what do I do with this?" and others of a similar nature.

To maintain this balance we suggest that it is beneficial to switch the order of presentation *of the session*. While the structure of the chapter provides a logical and orderly exposition from a "reading" point of view, for running the session a reversal may be more appropriate.

A brief lecture on Maslow's hierarchy of needs would be useful to begin. The hierarchy itself is familiar to most students of business administration, since it is touched on in most disciplines that deal with people. However, some useful discussion will arise when dealing with the possibility that the hierarchy may not actually work in other countries (see Pg 588, for example). This gives the students a general idea of how the rest of the session will be run. With this example in mind, the class may be split into smaller groups, each taking charge of one of the major motivation theories discussed in the chapter. They repeat the process of analyzing the model, and pondering its usefulness in an international setting. The groups then rejoin the class and present their findings to their peers in a general discussion.

The rationale for doing this in the first part of the session is that this may help to cater to the needs of the "now what" crowd by offering them concrete concepts, but along with caveats. Then proceed to discuss cross-cultural differences in leadership, in which case Discussion Question (1) would be a useful starting point. A good class assignment would be for students to do some prior research into cross-cultural management differences and present them in class, or as a hand-in project. The literature is replete with this kind of material, and students should have little trouble locating them in the library. Discussion Question (3) is a good end-of-session deliberation subject.

Overheads:

#1   What is Leadership?

A Vision
Inspiration
Focused Organization

#2   Motivation

Focus on need satisfaction.
Question is: Which Need?

#3   Maslow's Hierarchy of Needs

Self Actualization
Esteem
Belongingness and Love
Safety
Physiological

#4   Herzberg

Two Factor Theory:
A.   *Hygiene (lower-order)*
B.   *Motivational (higher-order)*

#5   McClelland

Dominant Need Groups:
A.   *Power*
B.   *Achievement*
C.   *Affiliation*

#6   Expectancy Theory

Exhibit 17.8, page 594

#7   Equity Theory

Input vs. Output
Compared with others
Motivation decreases with inequity

#8   International Applicability

No one theory warrants unrestricted universal application.

Discussion Questions:

1. Compare and contrast leadership in France with leadership in the Arab World.

    refer to Pgs 571-579.

2. In a country that is high on Power Distance, people generally expect and accept differences in power as appropriate. Discuss equity theory in the context of a high power difference society.

    students should refresh their memory on Power Distance by referring to earlier chapters (eg. Chapters 3 and 4). Equity theory and its implications can be found in Pgs 595-596.

3. Discuss the relationship of differences in leadership and motivation across cultures to the need for careful selection of expatriate managers.

    refer to Pgs 569-571, 584-585, and 596-598.

Test Questions

A. Multiple Choice Questions

1.   Leaders generally have a vision and:

   (a)   impose this vision on others.
   (b)   make sure they conform with cultural norms.
   (c)   inspire others to focus on this vision. (Pg 570)
   (d)   are willing to share it with whoever wants to join.

2.   Leadership is a quality that:

   (a)   must be examined in the context of the culture in which the manager operates. (Pg 570)
   (b)   all expatriate managers have.
   (c)   is based on economic success.
   (d)   all of the above.

3.   The most common approach for addressing motivation has been to:

   (a)   focus on the use of money as a motivator.
   (b)   focus on the satisfaction of needs of the workers. (Pg 585)
   (c)   delineate between hygiene factors and motivators.
   (d)   study the leadership traits of great leaders in history.

4.   Studies which attempt to analyze the universal applicability of Maslow's hierarchy of needs model:

   (a)   have concluded that Maslow's model is invalid in any context but the US.
   (b)   have found universal applicability.
   (c)   are not definitive in their support or refutation. (Pg 587)
   (d)   generally find a reversed hierarchy in Japan.

5.   Hygiene factors in Herzberg's Two-Factor Theory refer to:

    (a)   lower-order needs which lead to dissatisfaction if not present, but are not sufficient for motivation. (Pg 589)

    (b)   the use of money to provide for the worker's basic physiological needs.

    (c)   higher-order needs which must be satisfied if the person is to be motivated.

    (d)   the first stage of economic development when the population becomes more aware of hygiene requirements and thus are able to improve their lives.

6.   Herzberg's Two-Factor Theory:

    (a)   is valid in the US but not elsewhere.

    (b)   is valid in Japan and the US but not elsewhere.

    (c)   has not found clear support even in North America. (Pg 590)

    (d)   has found clear support only in North America, and only in the health-care industry.

7.   Which of the following is not one of McClelland's "dominant need groups"?

    (a)   power

    (b)   affiliation

    (c)   achievement

    (d)   socialization (Pg 591)

8.   McClelland suggests that individuals have dominant need groups which:

    (a)   they are born with.

    (b)   are acquired as people grow up   (Pg 591)

    (c)   are ranked in a hierarchy.

    (d)   are governed by whether the father or mother has dominant genes.

9.   McClelland's work has proven to be quite strong in:

    (a)   predicting assembly-line worker behavior in Third World countries.

    (b)   predicting professional worker behavior in Third World countries.

    (c)   predicting entrepreneurial activities and differences in individual need orientations across cultures. (Pg 593)

    (d)   predicting corporate manager's activities and group behaviors in organizational settings primarily in North America.

10.   Expectancy theory acknowledges that employees value different kinds of outcomes, and that:

(a)   **the manager needs to understand the expectancy mind-set of each employee. (Pg 595)**

(b)   people who value hygiene factors are more difficult to motivate than those who value motivators.

(c)   unless they view the outcome to be equitable, they will not be motivated.

(d)   the manager's job is to arrange these outcomes in a hierarchy so that they can be satisfied in order of corporate importance.

11.   The few studies that have been done on expectancy and equity theory internationally have:

(a)   raised doubts as to their usefulness.

(b)   **supported both theories. (Pg 596)**

(c)   been lacking in theoretical rigor.

(d)   shown their usefulness in France and Japan but not in the Arab World.

12.   A general observation can be made that:

(a)   motivation is impossible in a cross-cultural context.

(b)   host nationals should be hired whenever possible to manage the people in the subsidiary.

(c)   expatriates can never hope to acquire the skills needed to motivate people from other cultural backgrounds.

(d)   **need satisfaction is a useful focal point for motivation across cultures. (Pg 596)**

13.   Which of the following leadership strategies is not likely to work in France?

(a)   encouraging participation and employee empowerment.

(b)   emphasizing one's "hard-luck" childhood and how one had to struggle without an education and rose through the "rank and file."

(c)   de-emphasizing formal presentations and increasing the use of "management by wandering around."

(d)   **all of the above. (Pg 573)**

14.   Which of the following is not a common characteristic of "sheikocracy"?

    (a)   hierarchical authority.
    (b)   decisiveness in decision making. (Pg 575)
    (c)   patriarchal approach to leadership.
    (d)   nepotism at upper levels of organization.

15.   More than anything else, a leader's effectiveness in Japan is based on:

    (a)   the ability to work long hours.
    (b)   the person's past military record.
    (c)   the ability to understand and attract subordinates. (Pg 584)
    (d)   the ability to be part of the aristocracy.

B. True or False Questions

T (Pg 568)   1. The "universal" theories of motivation may not be universal at all.

T (Pg 570)   2. Leaders tend to be obsessed with a vision of where the group should go.

F (Pg 570)   3. Leadership qualities do not vary from one culture to another.

T (Pg 585)   4.The most common approach to motivation has been to focus on need satisfaction.

F (Pg 589)   5. Maslow's hierarchy of needs seems to apply across cultures, and the ranking of the needs do not change.

T (Pg 590)   6. The Two-Factor theory lacks empirical support even in North America.

T (Pg 593)   7. The manner in which the need for achievement is manifested is likely due to cultural norms and predispositions.

T (Pg 595)   8. Expectancy theory does not try to define or rank the specific needs of people; instead, the key is to understand what these needs are.

T (Pg 595)   9. Equity theory has to do with whether the person feels that his/her output/input ratio is similar to that of his/her coworkers.

F (Pg 597)   10. Expectancy theory is one of the least useful theories cross-culturally.

C. Short Essay Questions

1. Compare and contrast Expectancy theory and Maslow's Hierarchy in a cross-cultural context.

    refer to Pgs 586-589, and 593-595.

2. Attempt to relate the Expectancy theory with what you know about leadership in France.

    refer to Pgs 571-574 for discussion on France, and Pgs 593-595 for expectancy theory.

3. What is leadership, and what does it have to do with motivation?

    refer to Pg 570. See also Pg 584.

Appendix A

Careers in International Operations

Summary:

This appendix provides additional information for readers who are contemplating a career in international business or who are already in the field but wish to acquire additional skills and knowledge. The appendix begins with some insights into the prevailing cultural elements in several countries. The readers should not, however, interpret this to mean that these countries are by any means homogeneous with respect with their culture and the way business is done. The material in this chapter serves to alert the readers to some salient facets of management in an international context, but an in depth understanding of each society cannot be acquired without some first hand experience and much more involved research. For those who are considering a career in international business, this appendix provides some useful information regarding suggestions for *where to start*, as well as information on some prominent business schools (both in and outside of the US) which offer programs in international business. The listings are only meant as indicators that some researchers have arrived at, and should not be construed to be the ultimate truth. Indeed, whether a particular program is *right* for the individual depends largely on the person's objectives, background, and a host of other factors. Students interested in pursuing further studies in international business are advised to communicate to the schools concerned for more information, and to investigate other schools and what they have to offer. The appendix ends with a brief discussion on specialty programs that students may wish to take advantage of in their pursuit of an international business career.

Appendix B

International Management Experiential Exercises

Introduction:

Students may grasp the importance of international issues intellectually but need to experience the difficulties associated with international transactions personally; experiential exercises provide an opportunity for this personal involvement. These exercises also provide students an opportunity to test newly-learned theories and concepts and to make decisions in a realistic framework. Students find experiential learning especially helpful in terms of new attitudes, communication skills and self-awareness. This is particularly relevant in international management where these skills are critical to moving effectively from one country to another. Of course, practical knowledge of business is also important in the learning context. The exercises provided here have been designed to focus on realistic issues so they can be used to impart concrete business knowledge as well as new attitudes, communication skills and self-awareness.

These exercises are intended to supplement other teaching methods, including lectures, readings, case studies, research and computer simulations. A combination of teaching methods incorporates theoretical concepts with a practical understanding of the complex issues that international managers face. The exercises provide variety when used in combination with other teaching and learning approaches.

Experiential exercises take many forms. Some are completed individually, others in groups; some can be entirely conducted in class, others involve outside work; some take a few minutes, others several hours. The exercises provided here follow a number of different formats;   they are flexible in terms of class size, outside preparation and completion time.   There are guidelines regarding these issues, but each instructor will adapt these guidelines as appropriate.   The exercises here approximately parallel the issues discussed in the text, but experiential exercises often illustrate more than one idea.

Instructors should read the exercises before the course and decide which will be used, and when they will be used.   Advance preparation is a critical aspect to running these exercises successfully.   Having selected an exercise, consider the details of its administration to ensure that it will run smoothly in a particular setting - ie, is the class room flexible enough to allow the formation of small groups? is the class size appropriate for the exercise?   Two issues arise in using experiential exercises and should be considered:

1. Can they be used with large classes? Some are more difficult with large classes. It may be necessary to break a large class into several groups and have the exercise run in different rooms supervised by assistants.   Alternatively, the class can be divided into participants and observers, with the observers assigned the task of drawing "lessons" from watching the participants.

2. How does one ensure these are not seen simply as a "game"? The instructor can join various groups during the exercise to ensure that discussions are on track. It is important to follow an exercise by summarizing the lessons that should be learned from the exercise. This can be done by the instructor, possibly in the subsequent class; or, students can be asked to summarize and hand in the important points from their perspective.

If you are well-prepared, you should find that the exercises are fun and a valuable learning experience for both instructor and students. We hope that you will enjoy using them, and look foward to your feedback on their effectiveness.

EXERCISE #1   Risk Assessment and Management

CLASS SIZE	This exercise can be used effectively in classes of almost any size.
STUDENT PREPARATION	Each student is asked to do a preliminary risk assessment to identify three (3) potentially risky countries.
FORMAT	1. Divide the class into an appropriate number of groups, and have them follow the directions in the student text. 2. Have each group hand in their brief summary at the end of class.
TIME	**45 mins:** to divide the class and have the students complete steps 1 and 2. **15 mins:** to complete step 3.
PURPOSE	To consider assessing and managing risk where risk is seen as substantial.
GENERAL COMMENTS	The instructor may want to prepare a list of possible countries for the students to choose from. Possible suggestions are: **Mexico** **Romania** **Oman** **Brazil** **Sri Lanka** **Vietnam** **Columbia** **Egypt** **China** **Chile** **Russia** **Iran** It is possible that this list of countries can be used in other exercises.

EXERCISE #2   Cultural Scenarios

CLASS SIZE	This exercise can be used effectively in classes of almost any size.
STUDENT PREPARATION	None required.
FORMAT	1. Have students answer the questions and keep track of the answers. 2. Have students vote on the various options and discuss the appropriateness of the options.
TIME	**5 mins:** Answer questions. **20 mins:** Vote and discuss.
PURPOSE	To illustrate that the way we react "at home" to various situations may well be considered incorrect in other locations.
GENERAL COMMENTS	It must be stressed that there are no clear cut "right or wrong" answers.

EXERCISE #3   Motivation Cross-Culturally

CLASS SIZE	The class should be restricted to around 40 students. Classes of larger size may reduce the level of participation of some group members.
STUDENT PREPARATION	Read Chapter 17 or have familiarity with Organizational Behaviour issues.
FORMAT	1. Divide the class into an appropriate number of groups, and have them follow the directions in the student text. 2. Have each group present their skit.
TIME	**20 mins:** Divide into groups and complete step 1. **20 mins:** Develop skit. **15 mins:** Present skits.
PURPOSE	To consider the applicability of Motivation Theories outside the context of North America.
GENERAL COMMENTS	There is a danger that all groups may choose the same theory, so it may be prudent to make sure that each theory is covered by at least one group. This exercise should not be used until the material of Chapter 17 has been covered.

EXERCISE #4   Experimenting with Foreign Practices

CLASS SIZE	This exercise can be used effectively in classes of almost any size.
STUDENT PREPARATION	Read Chapter 3. Identify 3 to 4 practices from foreign cultures which are different from the norm at home.
FORMAT	1. Divide the class into pairs or groups of three. 2. Have them discuss the 3 or 4 practices they have researched. 3. Ask for volunteer groups to explain and demonstrate their practice. 4. Have every group experiment with this practice. 5. Continue until all practices have been explained.
TIME	**5 mins:** To form groups and discuss the practices. **The remainder of the class**: to explain, demonstrate and experiment with the practices.
PURPOSE	To try doing things in ways that are unusual for you.
GENERAL COMMENTS	There will be a tendency for the students to use the three examples from the text, so instructors are advised to have some practices ready for explanation and demonstration. This exercise should not be used until the material of Chapter 3 has been covered.

EXERCISE #5   International Strategic Choice: Country Analysis for Foreign Expansion

CLASS SIZE	This exercise can be used effectively in classes of almost any size.
STUDENT PREPARATION	Steps 1 and 2 must be assigned and completed in the class period before the exercise is to be completed. Steps 3 and 4 must be completed by the group before the exercise.
FORMAT	The groups are asked to present their analyses and they are subsequently discussed in the class.
TIME	Each group should be given 10 to 15 minutes for their presentation and 5 minutes for questions.
PURPOSE	To examine a number of foreign countries as potential sites for foreign expansion.
GENERAL COMMENTS	This exercise makes an excellent group project and groups may be asked to also submit a written report. The list of countries to be used may be drawn from Exercise #1.

<u>**EXERCISE #6**</u>   **Assessing Foreign Opportunities: Country Exhibits/ Presentations**

CLASS SIZE	If the class is rather small the exercise may be done individually. If the class is larger it may be divided into groups.
STUDENT PREPARATION	Students must prepare their presentation prior to the exercise.
FORMAT	**1.** Students or groups are assigned (or choose) a country for investigation and prepare a presentation. **2.** Students or groups then present their country to the class and discuss the implications.
TIME	Each student or group should be given 10 to 15 minutes for their presentation and 5 minutes for questions.
PURPOSE	To expose students to the business opportunities in a variety of countries and to consider how these opportunities relate to foreign-entry decisions.
GENERAL COMMENTS	This exercise can be assigned in lieu of the Country Poster. The list of countries to be used may be drawn from Exercise #1.

EXERCISE #7   Negotiations

CLASS SIZE	Class size is not a restriction unless the class is greater than 100 people.
STUDENT PREPARATION	Read Chapter 16.
FORMAT	Divide the class into three groups: Company A, Company B and Observers. Then choose two people from each group to form a Negotiation Scenario (therefore there will be 6 people per scenario). Assign each scenario a negotiation "scene" and have each Scenario follow the instructions in the student text.
TIME	**5 mins:** Divide the class into groups and assign scenarios. **10 mins:** Discuss assignment and prepare for negotiations. **30 mins:** Negotiations. **20 mins:** Reports.
PURPOSE	To illustrate the complexities of negotiating in an unfamiliar setting.
GENERAL COMMENTS	This exercise should be completed after the material of Chapter 16 has been covered. It is imperative that the instructor develop some scenarios for the class. An example of a scenario is: **LIBOM Oil Company is negotiating with CIAN Oil in China to set up a joint venture to manufacture automotive lubricants in China. LIBOM brings to the table the technology and additives for lubricants. CIAN brings a cheap source of labor and base crude oil. LIBOM wants to manufacture lubricants for what it sees as a huge market (China itself). It also wants to repatriate profits back to headquarters in New York. CIAN wants to acquire the technology to manufacture lubricants so it can eventually pull out of the joint venture and export lubricants itself.**

EXERCISE #8   Evaluating Subsidiary Performance

CLASS SIZE	Class size is not a restriction unless the class is greater than 100 people.
STUDENT PREPARATION	Read Chapters 10 and 11. Students should also have some familiarity with accounting statements.
FORMAT	Divide the class into groups and have them follow the instructions in the student text. Prepare the board with "Problems" and "Solutions" sections. After the students have written their suggestions on the board, the instructor then enters into a class discussion of the problems/solutions. Each group should have a spokesperson to explain their "problem" and "solution", then the instructor will invite comments from the other groups.
TIME	**25 mins:** Group preparation and discussion. **5 mins:** Writing of "problems/solutions". **20 mins:** Class Discussion.
PURPOSE	To illustrate some of the complexities of evaluating performance in different locations.
GENERAL COMMENTS	Much of this work can be done prior to class to free up time in the class for discussion. This exercise should be completed after the material in Chapters 10 and 11 has been covered.

EXERCISE #9   The Bata Shoe Organization and International Management

CLASS SIZE	This exercise works best with a small class.
STUDENT PREPARATION	None.
FORMAT	**1.** Divide class into groups and have students follow the instructions in the student text. **2.** Have students hand in written report or have students present their findings to class if time permits.
TIME	This exercise should take the entire class period.
PURPOSE	To explore, through an example, the issues involved in the globalization/localization debate.
GENERAL COMMENTS	Instructors may want the students to have read two articles to familiarize them with the globalization/localization debate: Levitt, T. **"Globalization of Markets"** Harvard Business Review, May/June 1993. Douglas, S. & Y. Wind **"The Myth of Globalization"** Columbia Journal of World Business, Winter 1987.

EXERCISE #10   Expatriate Assignments

CLASS SIZE	This exercise can be used effectively in classes of almost any size.
STUDENT PREPARATION	None.
FORMAT	1. Students will, individually, read and decide how they would react to the situation. 2. Divide the class into groups and have them follow the instructions in the student text.
TIME	**10 mins:** Consider the decision individually. **20 mins:** Group discussions. **10 mins:** Class discussions.
PURPOSE	To allow the students to take into account the variety of factors they must consider when approaching an overseas assignment.
GENERAL COMMENTS	It would be helpful for students to have some familiarity with Kenya in order to make their decision. If the class is rather large, the instructor may introduce other countries into the discussion (see Exercise #1 for a list).

EXERCISE #11   Cross Cultural Training

CLASS SIZE	A small class size is best for this exercise.
STUDENT PREPARATION	None.
FORMAT	**1.** Divide the class into groups and have them follow the instructions in the student text. **2.** Have students hand in their summary or have groups present their conclusions.
TIME	**30 mins:** Group preparation and discussion. **15 mins:** Group presentations.
PURPOSE	To consider cultural differences when designing training programs.
GENERAL COMMENTS	It would be helpful to prepare a "profile" of Anglo and Zetan characteristics. It should be stressed that these stereotypical Anglo characteristics are being used for illustrative purposes only.

EXERCISE #12   Facing Discrimination in International Assignments

CLASS SIZE	This exercise works best in smaller classes.
STUDENT PREPARATION	None.
FORMAT	1. Divide the class into groups and have them follow the instructions in the student text. 2. Have groups present their conclusions on one or two of the questions.
TIME	**30 mins:** Group preparation and discussion. **30 mins:** Group presentations.
PURPOSE	To alert students to issues related to discrimination which may arise when dealing with countries outside of North America.
GENERAL COMMENTS	Instructors may wish to ask: **"Is the definition of discrimination universal?"** It should also be noted that the purpose of this exercise is not to imply that the U.K. is a racist nation.

Appendix C

Selected International Cases

Case Notes:

Instructors who want to use case studies extensively will find excellent cases can be purchased through Harvard Business School and the University of Western Ontario, as well as elsewhere. There are also journals and texts devoted to cases, many with an international focus. Two case studies are provided here for those instructors who want to use cases less frequently, in conjunction with a variety of other teaching methods. These cases may be used for in-class discussion and/or assigned for written analysis.

Mitsuhoshi France, S.A. and *The Road to Hell* are both relatively short which makes them ideal for in-class discussion. These cases also illustrate many of the complexities of managing in a global environment, and this means they are equally suited to meaningful written evaluations. Each case deals with a specific situation which has far reaching implications for effective management and interactions in international firms. They could be used at almost any stage in the course, but we would suggest using one relatively early in the course, and one towards the end.

The Road to Hell would be especially appropriate early in the course. It incorporates many of the issues discussed throughout Part One of the text, including politics, culture and ethics. *Mitsuhoshi France, S.A.* would be most appropriate towards the end. This case illustrates many of the issues discussed in Part Three, including selection, training, managing the expatriate manager, and motivation of a multi-cultural workforce.

Case Summaries

The Road to Hell describes a Canadian subsidiary in the West Indies. John Baker, the Chief Engineer, is leaving the subsidiary after two years, and the case focuses on his final interview with his successor, Matthew Rennalls. Baker is described as a British expatriate with substantial international experience. Rennalls is the son of the Minister of Finance, and is described as very bright and well-educated.

Baker's major task for the past two years has been to groom Rennalls to take over his position. Rennalls is technically well-prepared and he relates well to local staff, but Baker feels he is overly race conscious and sensitive relative to expatriate managers. Baker and Rennalls get on well on the surface, but Baker feels that a barrier remains between them. In this final interview, Baker discusses these issues with Rennalls.

Mitsuhoshi France, S.A. describes a Japanese subsidiary in France. Legally, the subsidiary is independent, but in reality it is tightly controlled from Japan. Japanese expatriate managers hold the most important positions in France but have relatively little real decision-making power. French employees have little opportunity to advance and appear to find the Japanese environment somewhat difficult.

The case focuses on general issues associated with effective staffing in such an organization, as well as more specific issues associated with selection for a specific position, and motivation of individual employees.

Suggestions for Case Discussion and Use

The Road to Hell

The key to the discussion of this case is to identify and bring out the two different views of the situation. This serves to illustrate how politics, culture, ethics can all influence how a situation is viewed. An effective way to achieve this is to divide the class into two groups - members of one group take on the role of John Baker, members of the other group take on the role of Matthew Rennalls. The class is asked to prepare for the case by thinking about their role and preparing a synopsis of their view of the situation. In class, representatives for each side are asked to identify what they believe the letter in the in tray says.

The actual text of the letter - Exhibit I can then be distributed.

Class members can be asked to react to the letter from Baker's point of view, and from Rennalls'. This letter will usually lead to substantial further discussion of "who is in the right". This serves to illustrate how easy it is for us to see things in terms of right and wrong. The critical lesson is that no-one is right - rather different background and environments have led to cultural miscommunication. This is a good point at which to summarize the differences, and how these have influenced the communication process. The case discussion can then move to the following two issues:

      1. In retrospect, what could have been done differently to avoid this situation; that is, how can companies achieve cross-cultural understanding? How can multi-cultural diversity be managed to provide benefits?

      2. Given the current situation, what can be done; that is, how does one overcome cultural barriers to communication? How can cultural miscommunications be rectified?

If time permits, class members can role play a meeting between Baker and Rennalls and attempt to resolve the situation.

Exhibit I

Letter Text

Confidential

From: Assistant Engineer

To: The Chief Engineer, Caribbean Bauxite Limited

Re: Assessment of Interview between Messrs. Baker and Rennalls

It has always been my practice to respect the advice given me by seniors, so after our interview, I decided to give careful thought once again to its main points and so make sure that I had understood all that had been said. As I promised you at the time, I had every intention of putting your advice to the best effect.

It was not, therefore, until I had sat down quietly in my home yesterday evening to consider the interview objectively that its main purport became clear. Only then did the full enormity of what you said dawn on me. The more I thought about it, the more convinced I was that I had hit upon the real truth - and the more furious I became. With a facility in the English language which I - a poor Barracanian - cannot hope to match, you had the audacity to insult me (and through me every Barracanian worth his salt) by claiming that our knowledge of modern living is only a paltry fifty years old whilst yours goes back 200-300 years. As if your materialistic commercial environment could possibly be compared with the spiritual values of our culture. I'll have you know that if much of what I saw in London is representative of your most boasted culture, I hope fervently that it will never come to Barracania. By what right do you have the effrontery to condescend to us? At heart, all you Europeans think us barbarians, or, as you say amongst yourselves, we are "just down from the trees."

Far into the night I discussed this matter with my father, and he is as disgusted as I. He agrees with me that any company whose senior staff think as you do is no place for any Barracanian proud of his culture and race - so much for all the company "clap-trap" and specious propaganda about regionalization and Barracania for the Barracanians.

I feel ashamed and betrayed. Please accept this letter as my resignation which I wish to become effective immediately.

c.c.   Production Manager
        Managing Director

Mitsuhoshi France, S.A.

This case works well if one begins with general issues, and discusses specific individuals to illustrate the complexity of HRM decisions in international firms. The following can be used to guide this discussion:

1. From the perspective of the company as a whole, what are the major HRM concerns? How should company HR policies and practices be changed to be more effective?

2. From the perspective of a Japanese expatriate manager in France, what are your major concerns? How would you want the Japanese firm to change its HRM policies to deal with your concerns? Illustrate these concerns by discussing specific Japanese expatriate views.

3. From the perspective of a local/host country employee or manager, what are your major concerns? How would you want the Japanese firm to change its HRM policies to deal with your concerns? Illustrate these concerns by discussing specific host employee's views.

4. Based on these views, evaluate Mr. Takahashi's proposed new HRM strategy. If this new strategy is implemented, what obstacles will have to be overcome to ensure its success?

5. Discuss Suzuki's plan to hire a highly qualified French manager, in light of the previous discussion. How is Mr. Tanaka likely to respond? This scenario can be used to illustrate the obstacles above and to discuss in concrete terms how these can be overcome.

An option to a structured discussion is to begin by dividing the class into groups (the number of groups will depend on class size). Each group is assigned on set of managers to consider - Japanese expatriate managers or local French managers. Groups discuss the current situation and make suggestions for resolving it. After groups report to the class the following tasks are assigned:

1. Based on the above feedback, develop a staffing and training strategy for Mitsuhoshi.

2. In the context of this strategy, discuss staffing for the proposed joint venture.

The key element of this case is the need to accommodate a wide variety of personnel within an overall HR framework. The effective use of parent country nationals, host country nationals, and third country nationals needs to be considered, within the context of the overall corporate direction. There is much room in this situation for conflicts to arise - for example, effective use of one group may have negative implications for another or for control of the firm as a whole. This case provides a good vehicle for examining the realities of HRM decisions in international companies.

PART IV

TRANSPARENCY MASTERS

History of the Global Management Environment

1500 to 1850:   The Commercial Era

1850 to 1945:   The Explorative/Concessionary Era

1945 to 1970:   The National Era

1970 to 1990:   The Turbulent Era

Actors in the International Management Play

EXHIBIT 1.3

ACTORS IN THE INTERNATIONAL BUSINESS ENVIRONMENT

TWO-ACTOR STAGE

TIME PERIOD	World War II to 1955
KEY PLAYERS	Firm and foreign constituencies
CHARACTERISTICS	U.S. companies dominant National foreign investment policies in process of formulation U.S. viewed at forefront of management and technological developments

THREE-ACTOR STAGE

TIME PERIOD	1955 to 1970
KEY PLAYERS	Growing importance of host governments
CHARACTERISTICS	Countries newly independent Rise in nationalism Host governments sensitive to potential loss of power associated with foreign investment Japanese and European firms entering international arena

FOUR-ACTOR STAGE

TIME PERIOD	1970 to 1980
KEY PLAYERS	Growing importance of home governments
CHARACTERISTICS	Home governments seek to limit and prescribe appropriate company activities U.S. companies retrench

MULTI-ACTOR STAGE

TIME PERIOD	1980 onward
KEY PLAYERS	Special interest groups, international agencies, economic alliances
CHARACTERISTICS	Greater complexity. Need for awareness and assessment of changing global perspectives

Recent Developments

EXHIBIT 1.4

JOHN NAISBITT'S TEN "MILLENNIAL" MEGATRENDS

- Global Economic Boom of the 1990s - Free of the limits on growth known in the past, with an abundance of natural resources.

- Renaissance in the Arts - Arts will replace sports as society's dominant leisure activity during the 1990s.

- Emergence of Free Market Socialism - Eastern Europe heading in three directions: political pluralism, free-market economics, and, in the longer term, integration with Western Europe.

- Global Lifestyles and Cultural Nationalism - Intermingling of cultures to produce a homogeneous culture countered by small groups trying to maintain their cultural identity.

- Privatization of the Welfare State - A move from the welfare state to private ownership and private provision of services.

- Rise of the Pacific Rim - The role of the Pacific Rim countries in the global economy is expected to continue increasing.

- Women in Leadership - Women have reached a critical mass in the professions and business and their leadership role is becoming more important throughout society.

- Biotechnology - Rapid advances in biotechnology promise desirable changes but pose important ethical problems.

- Religious Revival - Religious belief is seen to be intensifying as it did a thousand years ago, and this is expected to influence all events in the coming decades.

- Role of the Individual - New technology, such as personal computers, fax machines, and cellular telephones, allows individuals the freedom to function on their own and thus make them less subject to societal pressures.

SOURCE:

From Megatrends 2000 by Naisbitt, and Aburdene. Copyright © 1990 by Megatrends Ltd. Printed by permission of William Morrow & Company, Inc.

Types of Governments

Capitalist

Socialist

Communist

Relating to Host Governments

MNC View
all things good

Captial for Growth and Development

Technology for Modernization

Skills for Local Industry

Access to Foreign Markets

Positive Contribution to Balance of Trade

Provision of Employment

Provision of Foreign Exchange

Tax Revenues

Development of Entrepreneurs

Host View
all things bad

Increased Dependence

Decreased Sovereignty

Increased Exploitation

Inappropriate Technology

Displacement of Local Firms

Outflows of Foreign Exchange

Mixed View

EXHIBIT 2.1

TYPICAL GOVERNMENT INVESTMENT INCENTIVES & RESTRICTIONS

INCENTIVES

Tax Holidays
Exemption from Duties
Tax Incentives
Monopoly Rights
Provision of Buildings
Low-Interest Loans

RESTRICTIONS

Local Ownership
Local Content
Local Personnel
Local Training
Location
Profit Repatriation
Foreign Exchange Use

<u>Categories of Political Risk</u>

Forced Divestment

Unwelcome Regulation

Interference with Operations

<u>Political Risk Management Process</u>

Step 1: Identify Risks

Step 2: Evaluate Risks

Step 3: Select Management Techniques

Step 4: Implement Techniques

Step 5: Evaluate Success

Step 1: Identify Risks

Country Characteristics

Type of government

Level of economic development

Stability of social systems

Stability of political systems

Company Characteristics

Industry

Technology

Ownership

Management

<u>Step 3: Select Management Techniques</u>

Defensive Approaches to Political Risk Management

Financial techniques

Managerial techniques

Logistical techniques

Marketing techniques

Integrative Approaches to Political Risk Management

Managerial techniques

Government Relations techniques

Financial techniques

"What is Culture"

"Culture is a learned, shared, compelling, interrelated set of symbols whose meaning provides a set of orientations for members of a society. These orientations, taken together, provide solutions to problems that all societies must solve if they are to remain viable."

"What is Culture"

* Learned

* Shared

* Compelling

* Interrelated

* Provides Orientation to People

<u>Cultural Underpinnings</u>

EXHIBIT 3.1

MODEL OF CULTURAL/NATIONAL VARIABLES & ORGANIZATIONAL BEHAVIOR

```
┌─────────────────────┐
│  Naional variables  │
│ (e.g., laws,        │──────┐        ┌──────────────┐
│  government,        │      │        │  Corporate   │
│  economy,           │      │        │   culture    │
│  technology)        │      ▼        └──────┬───────┘
└─────────────────────┘  ┌─────────┐         ▼
                         │ Societal│   ┌──────────────┐   ┌──────────────┐
                         │ culture │──▶│  Individual  │──▶│ Behavior in  │
┌─────────────────────┐  └─────────┘   │   values     │   │ organizations│
│  Societal variables │      ▲         └──────┬───────┘   └──────────────┘
│ (e.g., language,    │      │                ▲
│  ethnic origin,     │──────┘         ┌──────┴───────┐
│  religion)          │                │ Professional │
└─────────────────────┘                │   culture    │
                                       └──────────────┘
```

Cultural Underpinnings

1. *National Variables*

2. *Societal Variables*

3. *Societal/National Culture*

4. *Corporate Culture*

5. *Professional Culture*

6. *Individual Values*

7. *Behaviour*

Assessing Cultural Factors

1. Language

2. Religion

3. Education

4. Social Systems

5. Level of Development

6. Nation or Culture

Language

EXHIBIT 3.2

LINGUISTICALLY HOMOGENEOUS AND HETEROGENEOUS NATIONS

LINGUISTICALLY HOMOGENEOUS NATIONS

Albania	El Salvador	Jordan	Portugal
Argentina	France	Korea, North	Rwanda
Australia	Germany, East	Korea, Republic of	Saudi Arabia
Austria	Germany, Federal	Lebanon	Somalia
Brazil	Republic of	Libya	Sweden
Burundi	Greece	Malagasy Republic	Tunisia
Chile	Haiti	Mexico	Turkey
Colombia	Honduras	Mongolia	United Kingdom
Costa Rica	Hungary	Netherlands	Uruguay
Cuba	Iceland	New Zealand	Venezuela
Denmark	Ireland	Nicaragua	Yemen
Dominican	Italy	Norway	
Republic	Jamaica	Paraguay	
Egypt	Japan	Poland	

LINGUISTICALLY HETEROGENEOUS NATIONS

Afghanistan	Ecuador	Mali	Sudan
Algeria	Ethiopia	Mauritania	Switzerland
Belgium	Finland	Morocco	Syria
Bolivia	Gabon	Nepal	Tanzania
Bulgaria	Ghana	Niger	Thailand
Burma	Guatemala	Nigeria	Togo
Cambodia	Guinea	Pakistan	Trinidad
Cameroon	India	Panama	Uganda
Canada	Indonesia	Peru	United States
Central African	Iran	Philippines	USSR
Republic	Iraq	Romania	Upper Volta
Chad	Israel	Senegal	Vietnam
Congo	Ivory Coast	Sierra Leone	Yugoslavia
Cyprus	Laos	South Africa	Zaire
Czechoslovakia	Liberia	Spain	
Dahomey	Malaysia	Sri Lanka	

SOURCE:
Arthur S. Banks and Robert B. Textor. *A Cross-Polity Survey.* Cambridge, MA: M.I.T. Press, 1963, pp. 72–75; and World Bank Atlas, 1983.

EXHIBIT 3.3 .

SUMMARY OF FESTIVALS 1993

ABORIGINAL PEOPLES

June 21	First Nations Solidarity Day

BAHA'I FAITH

March 2-20	The 19-Day Fast
March 21	Naw Ruz
April 21-May 2	The Feast of Ridvan
May 23	The Declaration of the Bab
May 29	The Ascension of Bahá'u'lláh
July 9	The Martyrdom of the Bab
October 20	The Birth of the Bab
November 12	The Birth of Bahá'u'lláh
November 26	The Day of the Covenant
November 28	The Ascension of 'Abdu'l-Bahá

BUDDHISM

The following list of festivals has been devised by the Buddhist Council of Canada. It includes mainly those celebrations which are common to both Theravadins and Mahayanists; (M) indicates festivals more important to the Mahayana school, (Th) to the The ravada School. In the Western world, festivals are generally celebrated on the Sunday nearest the actual date.

January 23	Chinese/Vietnamese New Year (4691) (Year of the Cock) (M)
March 21	Spring Ohigon (Canada) (Japanese)
April 13-14	Saka New Year (Th) (Burmese, Laotian, Cambodian, Sri Lankan)
May 6	Wesak (Th, M)
July 3	Wassa (Th, M)
July 9	Dhamma Day (Th, M)
August 2	Ullambana (M)
September 21	Fall Ohigon (Canada) (Japanese)
September 30	Pavarana (Th, M)
October 16	Founder's Day (Canadian)
October 30	Kathina (Th)

HINDUISM

January 14	Makar Sankranti
January 28	Vasanta Panchami
February 20	Mahashivaratri
March 8	Holi (last day)
April 1	Ramanavami
April 13	Vaisakhi
August 2	Raksha Bandhan
August 11	Sri Krishna Jayanti
October 4	Ganesh Chaturthi
October 24	Dassehra
November 13	Diwali

ISLAM

January 19	Maraj-un-Nabi (begins in evening)
February 6	Nisfu-Shabaan (begins in evening)
February 23	First of Ramadan
March 20	Lailat-ul-Qadr (begins in evening)
March 24	Eid-ul-fitr
May 31	Day of Hajj (Day at Arafat)
June 1	Eid-ul-Adha
June 21	First of Muharram (New Year's Day, 1414 A.H.)
June 30	Ashura
August 29	Maulud-un-Nabi (begins in evening)

JAINISM

April 4	Mahavira-jayanti
April 24	Akshaya-tritiya
August 15	Paryushana-parva (Shvetambara sect)
August 22	Dashalakshani-parva (Digambara sect)
August 22	Samvatsari
August 31	Ananta-chaturdasi
September 1	Ksamavani
October 13	Mahavira Nirvana

EXHIBIT 3.3 (continued)

October 28	Lokashah Jayanti
November 23	Maunajiyaras

CHRISTIANITY

*   Julian Calendar
**   Gregorian Calendar
*** Both Julian and Gregorian Calendars

January 6	Epiphany**; Armenian Christmas
January 18-25	Week of Prayer for Christian Unity
January 24-31	Week of Prayer for Christian Unity (Canada)
February 24	Ash Wednesday**
March 1	Lent Monday*
March 5	World Day of Prayer
April 4-10	Holy Week (**)
April 4	Palm Sunday**
April 8	Maundy Thursday**
April 9	Good Friday**
April 11	Easter**
April 11-17	Holy Week*
April 11	Palm Sunday*
April 15	Holy Thursday*
April 16	Holy Friday*
April 18	Pascha*
May 20	Ascension**
May 27	Ascension*
May 30	Pentecost**
June 6	Pentecost*
August 6	Transfiguration Day**
August 19	Transfiguration Day*
October 3	World Communion Sunday
November 28	First Sunday of Advent**
December 25	Christmas**

JUDAISM

March 7	Purim
April 6-13	Pesach
April 18	Yom ha-Shoah
May 26-27	Shavuot
September 16-17	Rosh Hashanah
September 25	Yom Kippur
September 30-October 7	Sukkot
October 8	Simhat Torah
December 9-16	Hanukkah

SIKHISM

January 6	Birthday of Guru Gobind Singh
April 13	Baisakhi
June 2	Martyrdom of Guru Arjan Dev
August 28	Parkash
November 11	Birthday of Guru Nanak Dev
December 1	Martyrdom of Guru Tegh Bahadur

ZOROASTRIANISM

March 16-20	Ghambar hamaspathmaedem
March 21	Naw Ruz (New Year's Day in Fasli calendar)
March 26	Birthday of Prophet Zarathustra
April 30-May 4	Ghambar Maidyozarem
June 29-July 3	Ghambar Maidyoshem
August 13-22	Fravardeghan Days
August 23	Naw Ruz (New Year's Day in Shenshai calendar)
September 12-16	Ghambar Paitishem
October 12-16	Ghambar Ayathrem
December 26	Death of Prophet Zarathustra
December 31-January 4	Ghambar Maidyarem

The World's Most Common Religions

* *Hinduism*

* *Buddhism*

* *Islam*

* *Christianity*

Education

** Staffing Policies*

** Training*

** Level of Decentralization*

Social Systems

*   *Courting and Marriage Rituals*

*   *Entertaining Practices*

*   *Interaction of "Classes"*

*   *Kinship Units*

*   *Business Ownership*

Level of Development

1. Third World

2. Less Developed Countries (LDC)

3. Developing Countries

4. Newly Industrializing Countries (NIC)

5. Centrally Planned Economies

6. Developed/Industrialized Countries

Dr. Deming's Fourteen Points

1.   Achieve constancy of purpose

2.   Learn a new philosophy

3.   Do not depend on mass inspections

4.   Reduce the number of vendors

5.   Recongnize two sources of faults:

** management and production systems
** production workers

6.   Improve on-the-job training

7.   Improve supervision

8.   Drive out fear

9.   Improve communication

10. Eliminate fear

11. Consider work standards carefully

12. Teach statisical methods

13. Encourage new skills

14. Use statisical knowledge

What is business ethics?

Business Ethics:

The moral principles and standards that guide behavior in the world of business.

Key Concepts in International Business Ethics

Individual Relativism:

There is no absolute. The individual decides.

Cultural Relativism:

"When in Rome…"

Universalism:

"My way or the highway"

What is Strategy?

STRATEGY:

Critical Decisions

SWOT

Create Advantage

Avoid Disadvantage

Far-Reaching Effects

Integration Strategy (A)

When Appropriate?

Large Economies of Scale

Product Standardization

Low Tariff and Barriers

High Factor Cost Differences

Integration Strategy (B)

When Less Attractive?

Varied Consumer Preference

Limited Economies of Scale

<u>Strategic Objectives</u>

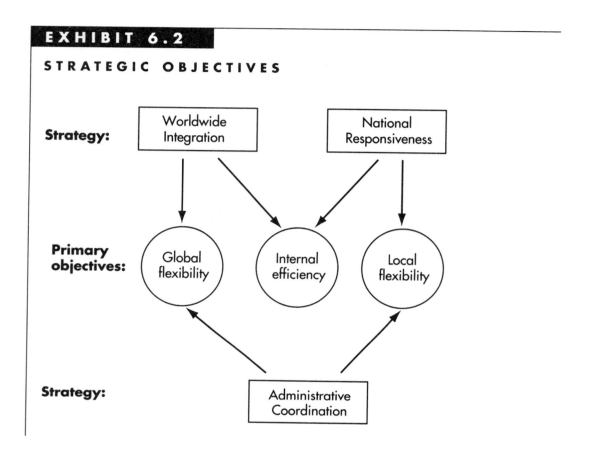

<u>Generic Strategies</u>

Cost Leadership

Differentiation

Focus

<u>Global Strategies</u>

Broad Line Global

Global Focus

National Focus

Protected Niche

Competitive Strategies Framework

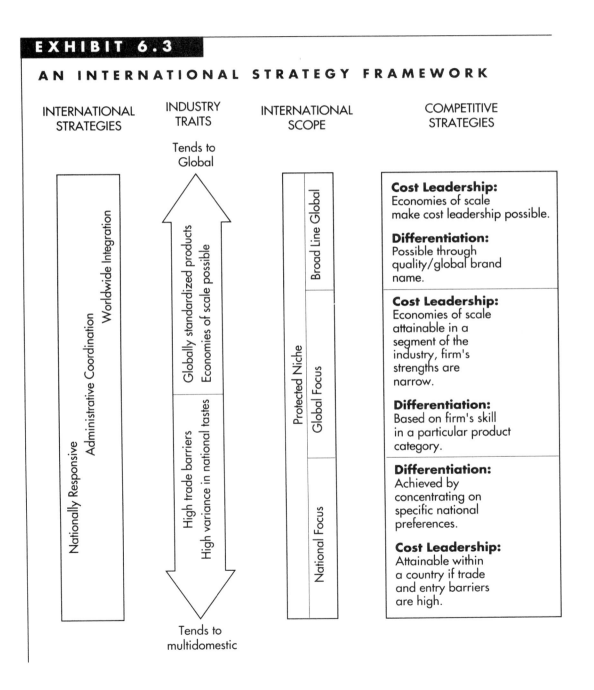

Organization Structure to Come

Decentralized Functions Across Subs

Increasingly Strategic Role for Subs

Multiple Structures used

Integrated Operations

Reacting to the Environment

EXHIBIT 7.1

SUMMARY OF REACTIVE REASONS FOR EXPANDING BUSINESS INTERNATIONALLY

OUTSIDE OCCURRENCE	EXPLANATION OF REACTION
Trade barriers	Restrictive trade practices can make exports to foreign markets less attractive; local operations in foreign locations thus become more attractive.
International customers	If a company's customer base becomes international and the company wants to continue to serve it, local operations in foreign locations may be necessary.
International competition	If a company's competitors become international and the company wants to remain competitive, foreign operations may be necessary.
Regulations	Regulations and restrictions imposed by the home government may increase the cost of operating at home; it may be possible to avoid these by establishing foreign operations.
Chance	Unexpected events can prompt a company to enter foreign locations.

Seeking Competitive Advantage

EXHIBIT 7.2
SUMMARY OF PROACTIVE REASONS FOR INTERNATIONAL BUSINESS

ADVANTAGE/OPPORTUNITY	EXPLANATION OF ACTION
Additional resources	Various inputs, including natural resources, technologies, skilled personnel, and materials may be obtained more readily outside the home country.
Lower costs	Various costs, including labor, materials, transport, and financing may be lower outside the home country.
Incentives	Various incentives may be available from the host government or the home government to encourage foreign investment in specific locations.
New, expanded markets	New and different markets may be available outside the home country; excess resources, including management, skills, machinery, and money can be utilized in foreign locations.
Exploitation of firm specific strengths	Technologies, brands, and recognized names are advantages that can provide opportunities in foreign locations.
Taxes	Differing corporate tax rates and tax systems in different locations provide opportunities for companies to maximize their after-tax worldwide profits.
Economies of scale	National markets may be too small to support efficient production, while sales from several, combined, allow for larger-scale production.
Synergy	Operations in more than one national environment provide opportunities to combine benefits from one location with another which is impossible without both of them.
Power and prestige	The image of being international may increase a company's power and prestige and improve its domestic sales and relations with various stakeholder groups.
Protect home market through offense in competitor's home	A strong offense in a competitor's market can put pressure on the competitor that results in a pull back from foreign activities to protect itself at home.

Foreign Entry Decision Making Process

Question 1Must we be more international?

Question 2Should we become more international?

Question 3Are we capable of becoming more international?

Question 4How can we improve our capability?

Question 5What specific opportunities do we pursue?

Question 6How should we enter a specific location?

Foreign Entry Choices

* *Exporting*

* *Licensing*

* *Franchising*

* *Contracts*

* *Turnkey Operations*

Export Intermediary Options

(i)   Direct from Exporter to Foreign Buyer

*(ii)   From Exporter, through a Domestic Export Intermediary,
to Foreign Buyer*

*(iii)   From Exporter, through a Foreign Import Intermediary, to
Foreign Buyer*

*(iv)   From Exporter, through Domestic Export Intermediary,
to Buyer*

Direct from Exporter to Foreign Buyer

Benefits

costs minimized

direct communication

internal export skills

familiarity with export markets

dominance of exporter's interest

Drawbacks

require internal specialists

cost of internal specialists

financial risk

From Exporter, through a Domestic Export Intermediary, to Foreign Buyer

Benefits

outside expertise utilized

good working relationships

free up internal resources

transfer of financial risk

Drawbacks

conflict of interests

no development of internal expertise

cost of intermediary

lack of in-depth knowledge

From Exporter, through a Foreign Import Intermediary, to Foreign Buyer

Benefits

specialized knowledge provided

intermediary has contacts

Drawbacks

communication barriers

provide export expertise

cost of intermediary

From Exporter, through Domestic Export Intermediary, to Buyer

<u>Transportation Issues</u>

* *Air*

* *Land*

* *Sea*

Payment Methods

* *Currency*

* *Credit*

__Documentation__

* Bills of Lading

* Commercial Invoices

* Export Licences

* Insurance Certificates

* Certificates of Product Origin

* Inspection Certificates

* Payment Documents

Ownership Options

(i)   Total Ownership

(ii) Public Sale of Shares

(iii) Ownership Fadeout

(iv) Joint Ventures

<u>Cultural Values</u>

Values

Needs

Attitudes

Norms

Hofstede's Value Survey Model (VSM)

4 Dimensions

Individualism (IDV)

Uncertainty voidance (UAI)

Power Distance(PDI)

Masculinity(MAS)

Kluckhohn and Strodtbeck's Value Orientation Model

Common Problem Areas

Relationship to Nature

Time Orientation

Basic Human Nature

Activity Orientation

Human Relationships

Country Clusters

EXHIBIT 9.4

COUNTRY CLUSTERS BASED ON EMPLOYEE ATTITUDE

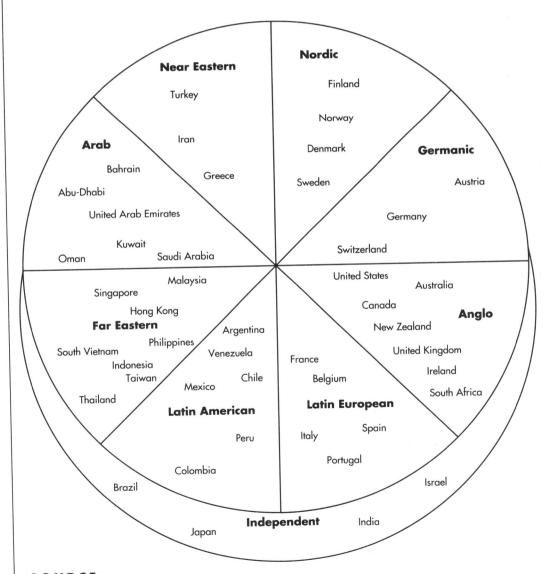

SOURCE:
S. Ronen and O. Shenkar. 1985. "Clustering countries on attitudinal dimensions: A review and synthesis." *Academy of Management Review*. Vol. 10, No. 3.

Country Clusters

EXHIBIT 9.6

RELATIVE SIMILARITY OF COUNTRY CLUSTERS TO ANGLO

Cluster 1 — Anglo

Canada, Australia, New Zealand, United Kingdom, United States

Cluster 2 — Germanic

Austria, Germany, Switzerland

Cluster 3 — Latin European

Belgium, France, Italy, Portugal, Spain

Cluster 4 — Nordic

Denmark, Finland, Norway, Sweden

Cluster 5 — Latin American

Argentina, Chile, Colombia, Mexico, Peru, Venezuela

Cluster 6 — Near Eastern

Greece, Iran, Turkey

Cluster 7 — Far Eastern

Hong Kong, Indonesia, Malaysia, Philippines, Singapore, South Vietnam, Taiwan

Cluster 8 — Arab

Bahrain, Kuwait, Saudi Arabia, United Arab Emirates

Independent (not closely related to other countries)

Japan, India, Israel

SOURCE:

B.J. Punnett. *Experiencing International Management* (Boston: PWS-KENT, 1989), p. 17. Used with permission. Based on information presented by S. Ronen. 1984. *Comparative and International Management*. (New York: John Wiley & Sons, Inc.).

Degree of Integration

EXHIBIT 10.1

SOME MAKE-VERSUS-BUY TRADE-OFFS

	MAKE	BUY
ADVANTAGES	Control over costs	Increased choice
	Control over quality	Business risks down
	Control over delivery	No additional investment
	Manage supply	No need for expertise
	Develop new expertise	
DRAWBACKS	Investment increases	Relies on outsiders
	Need for expertise	Competing for supplies
	Need for management	Supplier may go out of business
	May be inefficient	Overspecialization

Total Quality Management　(TQM)

"The international firm achieves TQM by identifying both similarities and distinctions in its worldwide operations and uses these to create quality"

Location of Facilities

	BENEFITS	COSTS
Concentrated	efficiency	reliance on one location
	standardization	
Dispersed	adaptation	high per-unit costs
	flexibility	increased adminstrative complexity

<u>Types of Facilities</u>

Climatic

Cultural

Physical

Governmental

Development of North American International Companies

Export Structures

International Division

Global Structure

Multi-Dimensional Structure

Export Structures

EXHIBIT 11.1

STRUCTURE INCORPORATING EXPORTS

		CEO		
Marketing & Sales	Operations	R&D		Finance & Admin.
				Exports

		CEO	
Paper Cups	Laundry Detergent	Light Bulbs	
			Exports

International Division

EXHIBIT 11.2
STRUCTURE INCORPORATING
INTERNATIONAL DIVISION

CEO

Product A   Product B   Product C   International Division

Global Structure

EXHIBIT 11.3			
GLOBAL REGIONAL STRUCTURE			
CEO			
North America	South East Asia	Africa	Europe

Types of Global Structures

Global Functional Structure

Global Product Structure

Global Area Structure

Characteristics of an Effective Control System

       i.   Accuracy

      ii. Timeliness

     iii. Objectivity

      iv. Acceptability

      v.   Understandability

     vi. Cost Effectiveness

    vii. Firm Specificity

Control System Basic Steps

Decide Final Results

Identify Interim Results

Establish Standards

Collect Data

Compare to Standards

Identify Deviation Causes

Corrective Action

Compare Actuals to Expectations

Review Plans and Goals

Control Mechanisms

Accounting

Auditing

Plans

Procedures

Policies

Bureaucracy

Corporate Culture

Centralization

Decentralization

Centralization versus Decentralization

Industry Factors

Type of Subsidiary

Functional Factors

Parent Philosophy

Parent Confidence in Subsidiary

Cultural Similarity

Firm Specific Advantage

Types of International Employees

Parent Country Nationals

Host Country Nationals

Third Country Nationals

Expatriates

International Adjustment

The degree to which the expatriate feels comfortable living and working in the host culture.

Culture Shock Cycle

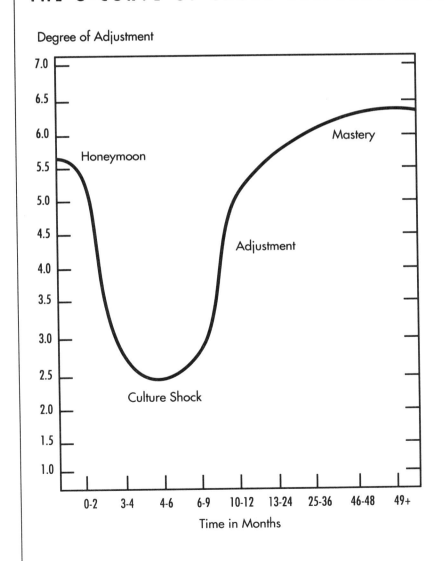

EXHIBIT 12.1

THE U-CURVE OF CROSS-CULTURAL ADJUSTMENT

Degree of Adjustment

Honeymoon

Mastery

Adjustment

Culture Shock

Time in Months

Framework of International Adjustment

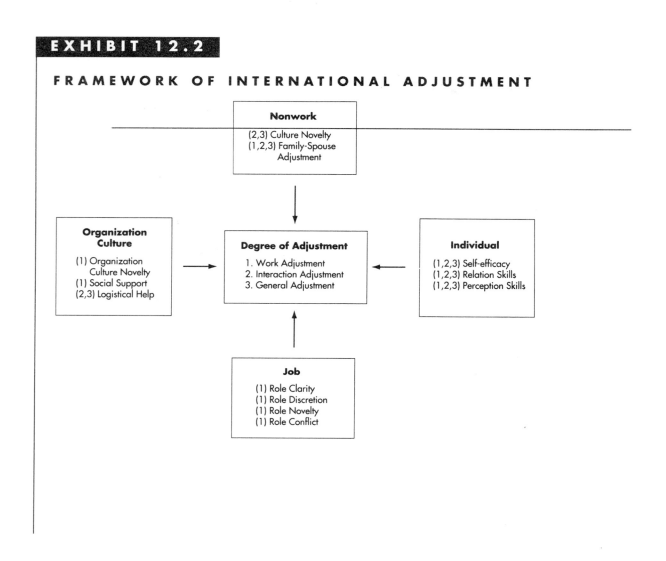

Framework of International Adjustment

Degree of Adjustment

1. Work Adjustment

2. Interaction Adjustment

3. General Adjustment

Framework of International Adjustment

Non-work

(2,3) Culture Novelty
(1,2,3) Family-Spouse Adjustment

Framework of International Adjustment

Individual

(1,2,3) Self-Efficacy
(1,2,3) Relation Skills
(1,2,3) Perception Skills

Framework of International Adjustment

Job

(1) Role Clarity

(1) Role Discretion

(1) Role Novelty

(1) Role Conflict

Framework of International Adjustment

Organization Culture

(1) Organization Culture Novelty
(1) Social Support
(2,3) Logistical Help

Training Method Selection

EXHIBIT 13.5

TRAINING SCENARIO

A   Level of Rigor: High
        Duration: 60-180 hours
        Approach: lecture, factual briefing, books, culture assimilator, role plays, cases, simulations, field experiences

        Training Content: Equal emphasis on job and culture. Stress job demands, constraints, and choices Include economic, political, historical, and religious topics

B   Level of Rigor: Moderate
        Duration: 20-60 hours
        Approach: Lecture, film, books, culture assimilator, cases
        Training Content: Equal emphasis on job and culture

C   Level of Rigor: Moderate
        Duration: 20-60 hours
        Approach: Lecture, film, books, cases, role plays, and simulations
        Training Content: Strong emphasis on job demands, constraints, and choices; less on culture

D   Level of Rigor: Low to moderate
        Duration: 20-40 hours
        Approach: Lecture, factual briefing, cases
        Training Content: Strong emphasis on job but little emphasis on culture

E   Level of Rigor: Moderate
        Duration: 40-80 hours
        Approach: Lecture, films, books, culture assimilator, cases, role play, simulation
        Training Content: Little emphasis on job; most emphasis on culture, including economic, political, historical, and religious aspects

F   Level of Rigor: Low to moderate
        Duration: 20-60 hours
        Approach: Lectures, films, books, cases
        Training Content: Little emphasis on job more emphasis on culture

G   Level of Rigor: Low to moderate
        Duration: 30-60 hours
        Approach: Lecture, films, books, cases, role plays
        Training Content: Little emphasis on job but more emphasis on culture

H   Level of Rigor: Low
        Duration: 4-8 hours
        Approach: Lecture, films, books
        Training Content: Little emphasis on either job or culture

Training Scenarios

EXHIBIT 13.5

TRAINING SCENARIO

A   Level of Rigor: High
        Duration: 60-180 hours
        Approach: lecture, factual briefing, books, culture assimilator, role plays, cases, simulations, field experiences

    Training Content: Equal emphasis on job and culture. Stress job demands, constraints, and choices Include economic, political, historical, and religious topics

B   Level of Rigor: Moderate
        Duration: 20-60 hours
        Approach: Lecture, film, books, culture assimilator, cases
    Training Content: Equal emphasis on job and culture

C   Level of Rigor: Moderate
        Duration: 20-60 hours
        Approach: Lecture, film, books, cases, role plays, and simulations
    Training Content: Strong emphasis on job demands, constraints, and choices; less on culture

D   Level of Rigor: Low to moderate
        Duration: 20-40 hours
        Approach: Lecture, factual briefing, cases
    Training Content: Strong emphasis on job but little emphasis on culture

E   Level of Rigor: Moderate
        Duration: 40-80 hours
        Approach: Lecture, films, books, culture assimilator, cases, role play, simulation
    Training Content: Little emphasis on job; most emphasis on culture, including economic, political, historical, and religious aspects

F   Level of Rigor: Low to moderate
        Duration: 20-60 hours
        Approach: Lectures, films, books, cases
    Training Content: Little emphasis on job more emphasis on culture

G   Level of Rigor: Low to moderate
        Duration: 30-60 hours
        Approach: Lecture, films, books, cases, role plays
    Training Content: Little emphasis on job but more emphasis on culture

H   Level of Rigor: Low
        Duration: 4-8 hours
        Approach: Lecture, films, books
    Training Content: Little emphasis on either job or culture

Training Rigor

EXHIBIT 13.3

Length of Training	LEVEL OF RIGOR	CROSS-CULTURAL TRAINING APPROACH

CROSS-CULTURAL TRAINING APPROACH

Length of Training

1-2 Months+

1-4 Weeks

Less than a Week

LEVEL OF RIGOR

HIGH

LOW

IMMERSION APROACH

Assessment Center
Field Experiences
Simulations
Sensitivity Training
Extensive Language Training

AFFECTIVE APROACH

Culture Assimilator Training
Language Training
Role Playing
Critical Incidents
Cases
Stress Reduction Training
Moderate Language Training

INFORMATION GIVING APPROACH

Area Briefings
Cultural Briefings
Films/Books
Use of Interpreters
"Survival-level" Language Training

LOW   MODERATE   HIGH

DEGREE OF INTEGRATION

Length of stay	1 Month or less	2-12 Months	1-3 Years

SOURCE:

Mendenhall, M. & Oddou, G. 1986. "Acculturation profiles of expatriate managers: implications for cross-cultural training programs." *Columbia Journal of World Business*. Winter, pp. 73-79.

The Dual Loyalty Paradox

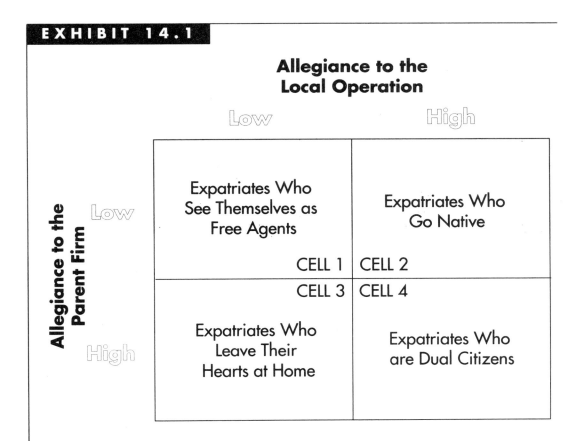

EXHIBIT 14.1

Allegiance to the Local Operation

	Low	High
Low	Expatriates Who See Themselves as Free Agents — CELL 1	Expatriates Who Go Native — CELL 2
High	CELL 3 — Expatriates Who Leave Their Hearts at Home	CELL 4 — Expatriates Who are Dual Citizens

Allegiance to the Parent Firm

SOURCE:
Black, J.S., H.B. Gregersen & M. Mendenhall. 1992. *Global Assignments: Successfully Expatriating and Repatriating International Managers.* San Francisco: Jossey-Bass, Inc.

The Believing, Yet Disbelieving in Stereotypes Paradox

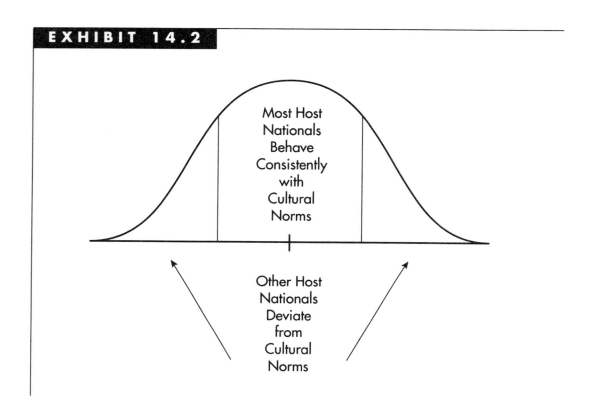

Fighting the Paradoxes

Overseas Support Systems

Integration Programs

Mentor Programs

<u>Overseas Performance Appraisals</u>

Factors of success for overseas operations

Input from the expatriate

On-site manager and former expatriate to evaluate

Repatriation Problems

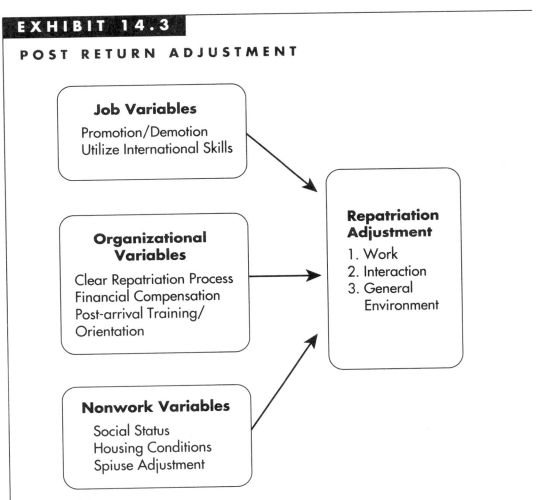

EXHIBIT 14.3

POST RETURN ADJUSTMENT

Job Variables

Promotion/Demotion
Utilize International Skills

Organizational Variables

Clear Repatriation Process
Financial Compensation
Post-arrival Training/
Orientation

Nonwork Variables

Social Status
Housing Conditions
Spiuse Adjustment

Repatriation Adjustment

1. Work
2. Interaction
3. General Environment

SOURCE:

Black, J.S., H.B. Gregersen & M. Mendenhall. 1992. *Global Assignments: Successfully Expatriating and Repatriating International Managers.* San Francisco: Jossey-Bass, Inc.

<u>Meaning of Equality</u>

A. Standardized, equitable treatment regardless of gender.

B. Differences exist, equitable treatment based on different contributions.

What do <u>YOU</u> think?

<u>Shortage of Women in Top Management</u>

*past discrimination

*present discrimination

*lack of interest

*lack of education and training

Five dimensions of Communications

1. Communication is a Process

2. Purposive vs Expressive Messages

3. Multi-Unit Signals

4. Context

5. Competence

<u>High and Low Context Cultures</u>

High Context:culturally homogeneous

Low Context:culturally heterogeneous

<u>Communication Barriers</u>

Ignorance of Cultural Rules

Perceptual Biases

Faulty Attributions

Stereotypes

<u>Negotiation: 4 stages</u>

Stage 1:Relationship Building

Stage 2:Exchange Information

Stage 3:Persuasion

Stage 4:Concessions and Agreement

What is Leadership?

A Vision

Inspiration

Focused Organization

<u>Motivation</u>

Focus on need satisfaction.

Question is: Which Need?

Maslow's Hierarchy of Needs

Self Actualization

Esteem

Belongingness and Love

Safety

Physiological

Herzberg

Two Factor Theory:

A. Hygiene (lower-order)

B. Motivational (higher-order)

<u>McClelland</u>

Dominant Need Groups:

A.   Power

B.   Achievement

C.   Affiliation

Expectancy Theory

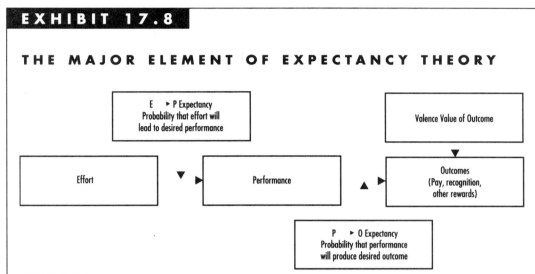

EXHIBIT 17.8

THE MAJOR ELEMENT OF EXPECTANCY THEORY

SOURCE:

Excerpts from *Management*, Second Edition by Richard L. Daft. Copyright © 1991 by The Dryden Press, reproduced by permission of the publisher.

<u>Equity Theory</u>

Input vs. Output

Compared with others

Motivation decreases with inequity

International Applicability

No one theory warrants unrestricted universal application.